MOTIFS IN ART AND LITERATURE

Proceedings of a Symposium held on the 8th of December 1984 at the Vrije Universiteit Brussel

Edited by

Michel VANHELLEPUTTE
and
Léon SOMVILLE

UITGEVERIJ PEETERS
LEUVEN

ISBN 90-6831-088-7
D. 1987/0602/32

CONTENTS

MOTIFS IN ART AND LITERATURE

ACKNOWLEDGEMENTS

Our grateful thanks are due to the Belgian National Foundation for Scientific Research (Nationaal Fonds voor Wetenschappelijk Onderzoek), which provided us with the main support for the organisation of the symposium on motifs in art and literature and for the publication of its proceedings. We should also like to thank the authorities of the Vrije Universiteit Brussel, especially Rector Oscar STEENHAUT, and the service for international cultural relations of the Ministry of the Flemish Community (Ministerie van de Vlaamse Gemeenschap) for complementary financial aid as far as the symposium was concerned.

The preface to the proceedings is essentially due to the patient work of Mr. Peter GEUDENS, who was the secretary of the «Werkgroep Motievenstudie» for more than nineteen months: we owe much gratitude to him for his virtually unpaid, but very competent assistance. Last but not least, we should like to thank Mr. Johan CALLENS and Mr. Frank WINTER for correcting the English text of the preface.

The Editors

PREFACE

The present volume, which contains the proceedings of the symposium «Motifs in Art and Literature», held at the Vrije Universiteit Brussel on 8 December 1984, acquires its full meaning only if situated within the activities of the «Werkgroep Motievenstudie», an interuniversity research group on motif study led by Léon SOMVILLE and Michel VANHELLEPUTTE, both of whom are professors at the Vrije Universiteit Brussel.

Owing to a lack of finance in the field of research on the humanities, the results of the workshop are usually communicated in preprints distributed in limited numbers (two hundred). Such preprints appeared in 1983 and 1985 under the respective titles «Prolegomena tot een Motievenstudie» (150 pages) and «Bijdragen tot een Motievenstudie» (120 pages). They consist mainly of theoretical contributions and case studies. In addition the «Bijdragen» contain the proceedings of a seminar held at the Vrije Universiteit Brussel on 9 May 1984.

A full grasp of the matters discussed at the symposium on «Motifs in Art and Literature» depends to a great extent on the knowledge of these preceding preprints. These are therefore included in the form of abstracts, arranged in the same order as the preprints themselves.

*
*   *

In his article, entitled *Theme, Motif, Matrix. A possible terminological parallellism between literary and artistic theory*, Paul Hadermann locates the notion 'motif' in art as well as in literature somewhere between the purely semantic and the purely formal level, because the motif — as he sees it — belongs to both spheres. He therefore tries to define it in contrast to the theme on the one hand and to what he calls matrix on the other. It has to be kept in mind, however that his intention is to attempt only a general approach and that, in practice, there may be dubious transitional and borderline cases between the three notions that he compares.

From a literary point of view he distinguishes between «theme» and «motif» as follows. He considers «theme» as a static, preliminary, self-constitutive semantic element. It has a clear-cut, conceptual meaning and may, as Ducrot and Todorov state it, «être présent (...) tout au long du texte et même dans l'ensemble de la littérature (le thème de la mort)». The author's intention may produce a theme in the form of a concept (e.g. anxiety), a myth (Prometheus), a topos (the striving man) or a fundamental image (e.g. «*Bezette stad*»). The theme mostly has a unilaterally denotative function. The motif — as a small «Bedeutungs-einheit» (meaningful unit) in a text — is far more restricted and concrete, for it may coincide with one single word or sentence and serve, together with other motifs, as a vehicle for one (or sometimes more than one) theme. But the difference between theme and motif does not in the first place lie in «leur degré d'abstraction, et, partant, leur puissance de dénotation», as Ducrot and Todorov put forward. True to its etymology, the motif is also a motor element pushing along the creative process — as well as the reception — not only in narration or in drama, in which it functions as the «motivation» of the action, but also in the lyric where it has the rather musical role of «leitmotiv», e.g. the leaf on the water in Gezelle's «t'Er viel 'ne keer», The «leitmotiv», for that matter, may also occur in the other two modes of expression.

In Hadermann's view, the semantic function of the motif is less strictly fixed than that of the theme. A motif may arise unexpectedly in the course of the writing process and receive its «meaning» only later on in the text or in a series of texts, e.g. through recurrence (leitmotiv). It is not even impossible that it should enrich, modify or even subversively derail the global sense of a theme or a complete work. The motif, being an open, versatile sign of a theme, therefore has a connotative function and, besides, plays a dynamic, structuring role.

The matrix, on the contrary, has no meaning in itself, but is a non-connotative, formal, almost mechanically repetitive element. Under this term Hadermann subsumes the idea of a hollow casting-mould with that of the «matrix», the womb enabling the genesis of new forms. Just like the motif, the matrix has a functional, sometimes «musical» value: it is meaningless in itself. It may coincide with a rhyme, an assonance, a rhythmical constant as for instance the phrase «this one was one» in Gertrude Stein's *Picasso*: «This one was one whom some were following. This one was one who was working (...). This one was one having something come out of him». It can also exist in a certain syntactic scheme which is consciously preferred or disapproved of by the writer. As an articulate utterance it provides mostly the basic rhythm or sentence patterns, the material for a motif. From its formal echo-effects and paronomasiae also emerge gratuitous images as in Max Jacob's poem *Comme un bateau* ...: «Dahlia! Dahlia que Dalila lia». Sometimes it is also used autonomously, as in the «Lautdichtung», nonsensical poetry, or «écriture automatique» (automatic writing). In some rare cases motif, theme and matrix may coincide, e.g. in *Soleils couchants* by Verlaine. Also, in the visual arts, we may distinguish between an abstract, preliminary theme — e.g. a notion like «war» or «vanitas» — and its rendering through either immediately recognizable or allegorical motifs. Those motifs have a semantic and a motor function at the same time. The artistic motif is also in a double sense structural and motor. Within one single work it may act upon the composition formally through the evocation of contrasts (naked versus dressed, flower versus insect, the smallness of man versus overwhelming nature etc.), through analogy (bottle and guitar, parents and children) or through repetition with or without variation (the nymph with the jar in Goujon's *Fontaine des Innocents*, the icebergs in C.D. Friedrich's *Die gescheiterte Hoffnung*, the identical female figures which are repeated smaller and smaller towards the horizon in Delvaux's *L'écho*). Within a global œuvre it will return as a «leitmotiv» or in series: Du Quesnoy's putti, De Chirico's mannequins, Cézanne's Montagne Ste Victoire, Delaunay's windows and Eiffel Towers or the squares of Malewitz and Albers.

There is often a geometrical scheme at the root of more strictly mimetic creations. Hadermann therefore considers it quite useful to call up the notion of «matrix» — as in literature — , in the sense of a small, purely formal unit whose role may be compared to that of the phoneme, the rhytmical constant or the recurring sentential pattern. If the motif has a referential function from its role as motor as well as a — albeit labile — semantically referential function, the matrix is again a meaningless structural element (curve, segment, corner, spiral or linea-forze) providing patterns for the genesis of motifs and of the global composition.

Klee, to whom the work of art is «in erster Linie Genesis», attaches an immense importance to such small elements, the combinations of which bring about the dynamics and the tension of the whole. But he calls them ... motifs.

Not only lines, but also colours may function as matrices, witness the multitudinous repetitions of the same vermillion in the jerkins of Brueghel's *Boerenkermis*, imparting rhythm to the whole surface, the way in which Delacroix emphasizes the lines of force of his compositions by white «reflets», or the pointillistic swarmings of neo-impressionism.

In short, the parallel terminology theme-motif-matrix seems, until further notice, to be useful in the comparison between literature and the visual arts. The theme, which is often one of the great commonplaces (love, death, struggle etc.) and which may receive concrete form in the image (myth, topos, history, allegory. fundamental image), establishes the semantic unity of the work and appears as a static invariant around which varying motifs rally.

The matrix, as a motor, formal unit, serves to build up the motifs through repetitive and variational patterns or, for lack of those, to establish immediately the structure of the work and the expression of the theme. The motif produces a connotative meaning and helps not only to illustrate and to shade the thematic aspect, but also to align the creative process and the structure dynamically by way of recurrence, variation and contrast, either in each separate work, or within a series of works. It plays a semantic as well as a structuring role and so it stands midway between the theme and the matrix. «Motivology» (just like «motivics», for the analysis of separate cases) fills up a gap between, on the one hand, the «thematological» study containing the general «Stoffgeschichte» and iconology as well as the exploration of specific themes of individual authors and artists and, on the other hand, stylistics, to which the notion «matrix» belongs. Thanks to the double function of the motif, semantic and formal-syntactic explorations enrich each other in «motivological» research.

In the essay entitled *Motif, shape, figure*, Annie Philippot-Reniers tries to assay the term «motif» with regard to the interpretation of modern painting. In her view, the problem of the motif in 20th century art can be linked to the more general problem of the increasing importance of the negative moment in the creative process, i.e. the moment, present in every creation, when the object is withdrawn from empirical space and time. While the creative consciousness has always managed to integrate this negative moment in the constituted image, which is characterized by a proper space-time-structure with a proper, autonomous presence, the artist, after Cézanne, has the tendency to hold back the creative process in the negative moment of the dialectic process.

The awakening consciousness of negativity was not formulated as such by an early modern painter such as Cézanne, and the first symptom of this phenomenon is the change which the term «motif» undergoes. «Travailler sur le motif», an Impressionist recipe, becomes with Cézanne synonymous of a real struggle, in which desiring, searching and going about become more important than achieving, understanding and comprehending. «Je tiens mon motif» becomes a momentary experience, the result of fitting together, entwining, and joining together formal elements. The motif becomes problematic; explicitly so for Kirkeby in relation to his own paintings and for Baselitz. With Cézanne it is apt to escape time after time and nowadays, since Pollock, it has an inclination to exist only as a bygone reality.

The discovery, and nowadays re-discovery, of the motif as an essential element and the recognition of its transitoriness change the whole creative process which, through its presence, proceeds in a broken, fragmentary but also more playful way. Precisely because the motif is the ever-escaping element, it becomes an object of desire and sometimes an obsessional object.

Through the technique of repetition a motif may grow into a *shape* (hence the series of works in which a motif, though insignificant by itself, acquires a mythical shape). When it is taken into account too consciously, however, it stiffens into a *figure*. It will reemerge in another, disobedient form...

S. Micha Namenwirth's contribution, *The motif in musicology*, has a distinctly exploratory character, being an attempt to define the various meanings the term has in musicological parlance within the context of its uses in the other arts. Issues touched upon are motif and narration, the musical motif as part of musical language systems, musical motif as a structural and as a referential term, the requirement that it manifest an identity of its own and draw attention to itself within a musical context, the historical interpenetration of vocal and instrumental motif types, motif and program music, the distinction between conventional and individual meaning complexes, the limited specificity of musical signs generally and the difficulty of making operational the motif concept in music (motif — theme — phrase — melody). Finally, the question is raised as to what extent the interdisciplinary study of motifs ought to be concerned with the musical motif in its referential sense (i.e. referring to extra-musical meanings), as opposed to its structural sense (i.e. as a basic building block in purely musical transformation processes). In *About the Motif in the Visual Arts* Jeanine Lambrecht works with Erwin Panofsky's motif notion. Panofsky labels as artistic motifs all the forms which may be recognized as carriers of primary or natural meaning. This boils down to a factual identification of pure forms as representations of natural or artificial objects (human beings, rocks, animals, plants, houses, tools etc.) and their mutual relations as events or situations. Within the *theme* representation (e.g. the Annunciation), motifs receive a *secondary* or *conventional* meaning: they become *figures* (e.g. a woman becomes a

Mary-figure) and are combined into *stories* and *allegories*. We therefore notice a certain similarity to the therminological distinction between theme and motif as it is often used in the study of comparative literature, i.e. the theme as the subject, the main thought of a work of art and motifs as smaller (formal) units which serve to construct the whole. Jeanine Lambrecht raises the question of how to take the plunge from motif to content. After trying to do so for the window-, door- and mirror-motifs in Dutch painting, she concludes that we are in need of a broader 'reading' than the one which is common in purely thematic iconography. The motif is first and foremost a self- constitutive entity and not a mere carrier of contents.

In his *Reflections on the Study of Themes* Léon Somville tries to set up a criteria study of the motif after having investigated thematics and interdisciplinarity. He arrives at the conclusion that the notion of «motif» may be defined either on the level of the content (hermeneutic reading by Richard an Riffaterre) or on the level of the expression (pragmatic reading by Genette). In the first case the following criteria may be distinguished: (1) recurrence (2) isomorphism (3) symbolism, to these may be added — intertextually — (1) stylistic mark (2) signifier function (3) productivity. In the second case the motif is subject to the criteria established by the poetic theory of genres. It is acknowledged as mimesis and not as semiosis: it is resumed, not interpreted.

Anne Marie Musschoot investigates the *position of the motif in narration theory*. Since the beginnings of present-day structuralist and semiotic narration theory the notion of motif has been treated as the smallest narrative unit. The Russian formalists have already pointed out that the motif in a story is a scheme which forms part of the overall narrative structure. V. Propp extended this definition in the notion of «function», which, however, as Doležel argued, cannot replace the notion «motif» altogether.

In modern literary theory the notion of motif is twofold, depending on whether the student takes the theoretical poetics or the historical poetics point of view. In the first case the motif is defined as the «smallest meaningful unit of a text« and viewed in a syntactic context, while in the second case the semantic aspect is focussed on. The division corresponds to that between the structuralist and hermeneutic approaches.

The manifest tendency in more recent literary theory to orient research pragmatically towards the discursive level (the verbal level) also finds

expression in the approach to the notion of motif. J. Lotman, e.g.,
describes the motif as a happening in which the limits of a semantic field
are broken for the percipient reader.

Joris Duytschaever contributed an essay *on the problematic Usefulness
of the Concept of « Matrix » for the psychoanalytic Study of Motifs*. The
status of the term «matrix» has been very precarious ever since its
introduction into literary studies by Scott Buchanan's classic *Poetry and
Mathematics* (1929).
Following up Paul Hadermann's attempt at a more rigorous definition
by using matrix as a conplementary concept to account for elements not
covered by the concepts of theme and motif, this essay explores the
concept's usefulness from the specific angle of psychoanalysis.

Although the concept does not belong to traditional psychoanalytical
theory, it can be introduced into this framework with a view to clarifying
a question neglected by Freud: where is the material of literary works
derived from, material in the sense of *Stoff* just as much as of *Thema* or
of *Motiv*?

If connected with the concepts of fixation and archaic conflict, the
concept of matrix can be used to explain the most fundamental formative
impulse generating motifs which can finally be subsumed under a general
theme such as «the Oedipus complex». Although according to some
contemporary analysts the classic division in oral, anal and phallic
phases is no longer clinically practicable, this does not imply that its
appeal to artists has become less powerful, as witness many works of art
which explicitly or implicitly derive their motifs and themes from these
basic driving forces, concurrently reactivating archaic conflicts in the
subconscious of the audience.

Taking his cue from a seminal essay by James Manley on «Artist and
Audience, Vampire and Victim: the Oral Matrix of Imagery in
Bergman's *Persona*» (1979), which identifies a matrix of imagery centred
on feeding (sucking, devouring, being devoured), leading to a complex of
oral motifs and generating manifest themes, Joris Duytschaever attempts
to illuminate several works of English and Dutch literature in which oral,
anal, or phallic elements are foregrounded.

Finally the problem of narcissism is raised, because it is not clear
whether it should be discussed in terms of «matrix» or in terms of
«theme»: like the oral, anal, and phallic developmental phases it is
categorically pre-Oedipal, but on the other hand it is closer to the
Oedipal in that it carries more substance in terms of traditional

thematics. Its ambiguous status will have to be clarified in collaboration
with professional psychoanalysts.

In the meantime, the concept of matrix can already be used produc-
tively to differentiate between various kinds of motifs.

Hans Werner am Zehnhoff presents us in *Migration of Motif and
Parody* with a fundamental reflection on the history of a motif which is
exposed by means of the picaresque. *Intratextual* and *intertextual* motifs
have a different historical range. *Intratextual* motifs have a rather short
history, since they are bound to the well-defined œuvre of a well-defined
artist. They are of interest in the fields of biography, literary criticism,
hermeneutics, micro-history etc. *Intertextual* motifs very often have a
much longer history. They have appeared, vanished and reappeared in
the social and cultural history of mankind for thousands of years.

Since it is difficult to retrace the origins of a motif H.W. am Zehnhoff
chose the picaresque, the history of which is relatively clear. In fact, the
picaresque motif appears regularly at a certain chronological distance
from the heroic motif, one of the standard motifs in the history of art and
literature. Whenever the high moral aspirations of the hero start to fade
away, the mock-heroic (picaresque) motif comes into prominence. This
phenomenon is illustrated by several examples from the history of
literature (Achilles, Ulysses, Encolpius, Amadis, Don Quixote, Sim-
plicius Simplicissimus, Schwejk, Oskar Matzerath etc.).

The heroic motif and the picaresque motif constitute an oppositional
pair. It seems that the appearance of this constellation is relevant, for it
marks important historical changes; the picaresque motif develops as the
parodic counterpart of the heroic motif and follows its own laws of
evolution.

The opposition between heroic and picaresque motif does not imply
the end of the heroic motif. However, am Zehnhoff can determine a
decline in its ethical standard because of the growing discrepancy
between reality and pretension; the history of the application and the
reception of the heroic motif continues at a lower level in trivial
literature.

There is no apparent law for the appearance of the heroic motif. But
the appearance of the picaresque motif marks the beginning of the
decline of its counterpart. The picaresque motif in turn fades away when
a new evolution comes to the fore.

The constellation of the pair 'heroic motif vs. picaresque motif' seems
to be rather constant and has no internal evolution. It is most likely that

parodic pairs of motifs, clusters of motifs or any kind of combination of motifs are easier to trace and to describe than isolated motifs.

Adolphe Nysenholc deals with *the Motif of the Watch* in some of Chaplin's films. This motif, at the heart of Chaplin's œuvre, not only personifies the hero (see *The Pawnshop*), but also represents comedy itself (timing + circularity); cfr. the revolving door in *The Cure*. The watch putting life into the hero is a motif in the etymological sense of «motor», setting the adventure of the film in motion (as in the beginning of *The Circus*, where the stolen turnip watch gives rise to the chase). The components of the story are engaged like the parts of timepieces. The watch, translating linear time into a circular space, is also a metaphor of the editing, and indeed of the shooting and the projection of a film.

Chaplin has his film in hand, through his watch: it even appears as a condensed projection of the whole cinema, with all the clockwork of this industry of the imaginary. Occasionally, Chaplin finds himself *in* the watch (as in *Modern Times*), or he is snatched into the «dream factory», ... and regresses to the womb where he rediscovers his first noise (the heartbeat of his mother).

The watch generates Chaplin: It is the mother-womb of both his being and of his works. It is a multi-stage motif, by resonance; a translation, in the Spitzerian sense, of an «etymon of the work».

In his essay on *The Insect-motif in the Work of Franz Kafka*, Michel Vanhelleputte explains that Gregor Samsa's metamorphosis is only the final stage of a development which must have started far earlier, that is, if it is not a mere coincidence. Though Samsa's responsibility for his becoming an insect is not very conspicuous at first sight, some critics — among whom the well-known philologists Heinz Politzer and Walter H. Sokel — think that this responsibility does exist. Their interpretations are undoubtedly interesting and largely correct, but they do not take into account an early story which was left incomplete, viz. the *Hochzeits-vorbereitungen auf dem Lande*. Its autobiographically tinged hero, Eduard Raban, sees himself lying on a bed as an insect. The presentation here was in fact optimistic: the metamorphosis seemed to promise peace and security. But the existential attitude which finds expression in this dream of becoming an insect, is not very different from Gregor Samsa's attitude towards his surroundings.

This permits us to attach a new dimension of depth to the basic motif of *Die Verwandlung*: becoming an insect reflects Kafka's inclination to seclusion, to escape from his fellow-men, «Stille, Dunkel, Sich-Verkriechen», as he himself puts it in a letter to Milena Jesenská. But what sharply distinguishes *Die Verwandlung* from *Hochzeitsvorbereitungen auf dem Lande* is the interpretation of the motif: what was earlier on considered as a blessing, seems eventually to be felt as a curse (at least from a worldly point of view). And we know enough about Kafka to realize that this is very closely related to biographical circumstances. We are here dealing with a philologically «inter-textual» but biographically «intra-textual» motif.

Sven-Claude Bettinger's article on *The Handsome Sailor* is a contribution to the interpretation of the motif of the sailor in a few literary works of the 19th and 20th centuries. The article presents an attempt to examine the notion of 'motif' more closely in the light of some practical examples. The notion should there become more accurately definable. As motif, the figure of the sailor was chosen because it appears regularly in the literature as well as in the visual arts of the 19th and the 20th centuries. The analysis is, however, confined to literary works. The motif of the sailor is examined in one poem or prose-work by different authors, from different countries and epochs, using different languages, so that conclusions may be drawn from as many different contexts as possible.

The following works are analysed: *Billy Budd, Sailor* (1891) by Herman Melville; *Der Tod in Venedig* (1911) by Thomas Mann; *Querelle de Brest* (1953) by Jean Genet; *Der Garten* (1963) by Hubert Fichte; *Wolf* (1983) by Gerard Reve; *The Obelisk* (1939) by E.M. Forster; *Teorema* (1968) by Pier Pasolini; *In memorian A.H.H.* (1850) by Alfred Lord Tennyson; *In Cabin'd Ships at Sea* (1892) by Walt Whitman; *A Mightier than Mammon* by Edward Carpenter; *Ode Maritima* (1915) by Fernando Pessoa; *Twee uitnodigingen* (1949) by Hans Lodeizen; *L'adieu aux fusiliers marins* (1917) by Jean Cocteau.

Bettinger's treatment of these works shows that the figure of the «handsome sailor» is one of the motifs in the approach to the theme of homoeroticism. As such it is static and in certain respects even archetypal, because it has been used at different times, in different cultures by different authors (also when there are traceable influences, for instance, from Genet to Fichte, from Whitman to Pessoa). The motif divides itself variably into a whole series of subsidiary, meaningful elements, each stressing impressions in a different way (e.g. the symbolism of the water, the colour white, the city of Venice or the garden in the sense of «hortulus animae»). In essence, though, these elements sub-

ordinate themselves to the general meaning of the motif. In another
context, however, they might appear as autonomous motifs throughout.

Daniel Acke critically examines the theory of the literary motif which
S.-I. Kalinowska puts forward in her book on the literary *motif in the
poems of Emile Verhaeren.*

By means of the conceptual apparatus she proposes, Kalinowska
intends to remedy the confusion existing in the field of research into the
literary motif. This enterprise, however legitimate, in fact reintroduces
the traditional analysis of contents and style under the cover of a new
terminology.

A priori, the perspective in which Kalinowska proposes to study the
literary motif is attractive. She claims to work with an exclusively literary
viewpoint. This means that the type of analysis she advocates focusses on
«the work in so far as it has become a product which is independent of
the creative subject». Thus, Kalinowska shows that she wishes to rule out
all psychologism and in so doing, she seems to join the current of new
criticism.

She, however, considers her analysis to be original because it takes
account of the aesthetic aspect of the motif (that is to say, its form)
whereas formerly, according to Kalinowska, studies were restricted to
either the motif as idea («Ideengeschichte») or the motif as topic
(«Stoffgeschichte»). In Kalinowska's view, the motif has a binary
structure like the linguistic sign. The motif is «a structural-limiting,
complete and autonomous element, that is to say, it is sufficiently
developed to have a significant meaning and a characteristic expression».
The motif therefore includes a designated element (the idea: «notions
and concepts, conceptualized emotional and volitional states») as well as
a designating element (the form: «morphological, syntactic and lexical
factors, images ...»). There is no literary motif without the unity of
concept and form.

Nobody will dispute the principle of the unity of form and contents in
literature. But in fact, Kalinowska's analysis gives a priority to the ideas.
Indeed, the motif's textual basis is generally a scene or a picture (in a
play), a chapter or paragraph (in a novel), or (in poetry) one single lyrical
piece. In a poem, for instance, a content (conceptual scheme) is always
expressed by a form (the motif in so far as it is signifier). As is also shown
by Kalinowska's work on Verhaeren, in this perspective the analysis will
consist in tracing the motif of the poem, — which is nothing but its
principal idea — and in looking for the corresponding stylistic expres-

sion. The concepts «formant» and «thème» indicating unities which are respectively inferior and superior to the motif from a purely quantitative point of view, serve only to introduce new distinctions on the level of the ideas (respectively secondary and more general ideas). Each poem therefore converges towards one unique sense and the style is only the outer cover, the exterior of the ideas. In the end, one finds the old intuitive analysis of literature in Kalinowska's work but in the meantime it has been unnecessarily burdened by a new conceptual apparatus.

Hendrik van Gorp wrote a *comment on the above studies* of the research group in terms of literary theory. He argues that on the basis of these studies a schematic representation may be discussed in which the terms «matrix» and «theme» are related to each other. The notion «motif» may be approached in two ways, each corresponding to a particular branch of literary theory. In historical-comparative, «thematological» analyses — which are by nature intertextual — the motif is regarded as a semantic unit which is repeated, with limited variations, in different works. From the structural-theoretical point of view, on the other hand, motifs are considered to be small, indivisible meaningful units within one work. The structural approach also distinguishes between dynamic motifs bearing on happenings and static motifs relating to situations. In the actual reading of a text, both dynamic and static motifs are conceived as the common features of divergent lines causing the different parts in the text to be perceived as a continual line, or at least as a whole. The reader clusters the motifs progressively so that they eventually come together in what may be called the fundamental or basic motif. The reformulation of the motif in metalanguage is the theme of a work. Thus the theme is the global semantic unity or, in other words, the idea or action which summarizes the whole.

To prevent the structuralist analysis from becoming mere sophisticated augury, one also has to concentrate on the semantic aspect of the elements, so that semiotics come into play. The shift from structuralist to semiotic approach implies that the meaningful units in a text are related to the reader's expectations and to the socio-cultural context. A given element in a text is never a motif by itself, but it may receive 'motif value' from a certain extra-text (culture) in a certain context. The same holds for thematology, but here the attachment of motif value is dependent on intertextuality. The text guides the reader in the discovery of motifs. Signals and criteria pointing to motif value are, for instance, repetition, isomorphism, topological and symbolical valency. A certain markedness or, at least, lack of necessity is also an indispensable feature of the motif.

In contrast to the motif, the theme does not have to be explicitly expressed in the text. The theme, being «a static, semantic element with a clear-cut conceptual meaning» (Hadermann) is a further abstraction of the motifs. The notion «matrix» stands on the other side of this abstraction. With regard to the contents of a work, «matrix» is the equivalent of «matter» («Stoff»), i.e. the geographically and historically determined subject matter, the raw material («Rohstoff») which may be worked up into motifs. As far as the form is concerned, the matrix is «an almost mechanically repetitive element which has no meaning by itself» (Hadermann). It provides material for motifs as well, but from a purely formal basis, and it includes rhyme-schemes, metres, assonances etc. However, Van Gorp thinks it better to extend Hadermann's definition to cover rhetorical and topical schemes, genre conventions and the like. Thus viewed, the formal matrix has to be understood as a conceptual scheme, a background pattern («Grundmuster»), a pre-existent empty structure which is filled up in a particular work of art. It comprises, for instance, the structural models of classic rhetoric as well as the conception of the 19th-century psychological novel. In this view, the image of the handsome sailor (Bettinger) and the picaresque 'motif' (am Zehnhoff) also have to be considered as matrices rather than motifs. Besides, the notion «matrix» may well be linked to Riffaterre's «hypogram», since it is a latent structure brought into being by intertextuality. This representation of the facts is equally applicable to intratextual and intertextual studies. Intratextual analyses have the purpose of showing how the notions «matrix», «motif» and «theme» receive a proper meaning within one text. Thematology, on the other hand, concerns itself with the transformation of one and the same subject matter into various, differing motifs. In this connection it is important to note that similar motifs may acquire completely different functions in different contexts.

All this may be represented schematically as follows:

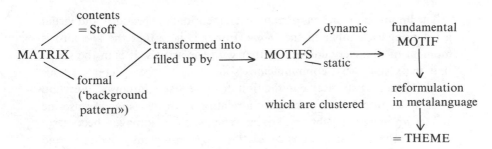

Alexander Van Grevenstein, who commented on the prolegomena from the point of view of art theory, holds that there is a large gap between the language of the visual arts and the language of art criticism. Art critics do not have the possibility of expressing their thoughts and feelings in the language which constitutes the object of their appreciation or disapproval. A literary critic uses words to talk about literary works which are made up of words themselves. An art critic has no choice but to use words as well, though the object of his criticism is made up of completely different materials such as light, space, colours, contrasts etc. So, according to Alexander van Grevenstein, art criticism should use a terminology which shows to better advantage the specificity of the visual arts. By its nature, such a terminology will be completely different from that which is applied to literature and music.

Let us take, for instance, Pierro della Francesca's painting showing — amongst other things — an egg hanging on a thread from an arch above a madonna and child. This odd egg summarizes the whole complex concept of 'Renaissance'. It cannot be described in literary terms. For it is not merely a symbol, a prefiguration, a theme or a motif, but first and foremost it is a shape, a 'Gestalt' harmonizing the contrast between art and reality in a paradox. It seems best to indicate the specific qualities of visual arts before examining the features shared with literary art. The structural analysis of the phenomenon 'visual arts» is not nearly so advanced as that of literature and music happens to be. Since we have known a babel of tongues for the past few decades, it is hard to translate the visual system at this moment. Art criticism must therefore focus upon the confrontation with the individual work of art. For each work of art is definitive and radical, each time there is a crucial moment, decisive as to whether one touch of the brush will turn the painting into a masterpiece or not. So, what matters is not the showing of a Rembrandt, but *this* particular Rembrandt, *that* particular De Kooning or Baselitz. An œuvre is nothing but the positive context of one or more extremely important works.

The important word has already been mentioned: spectator and visual artist meet each other in the *shape*. For it is here that the spectator's moment of discovery comes together with the artist's. It is in the shape that the visual artist communicates something to the spectator of his work. Visual artists receive in the first instance visual impulses: a certain light, space or colour. Looking for a relation to those visual impulses he creates an image of light and space. When such an «image» becomes a «shape», the highest aim has been attained. Consequently, «shape» and «image» are the terms that matter.

And what about the motif? The notion «motif» lacks substance with respect to the visual arts and is of no great help in their analysis. Precisely the visual arts of our century, so it seems, have done away with the illusion created by the notion «motif». This is clearly shown by Paul Klee's œuvre. In his early works, Klee, giving way to a need to rationalize, to legitimize the incomprehensible and the unpedagogic, reduced nature to a never-ending series of motifs. Only towards the end of his life did he manage to liberate the motif from literal and pedagogic duties, so that the unpedagogic and the unknown could appear. In other words: the motif made way for the shape. Sol Lewitt and G. Baselitz also showed the inapplicability of the motif to visual arts, each in his own way. Sol Lewitt paradoxically used repetition to lift the square out of the realm of motifs. Baselitz' conversion of the figure cannot be called a «motif» either, since he wanted to strip the image entirely of its iconographic value.

The motif is therefore linked to 'figure', or figurative art. It is a constituent part of iconography. Unfortunately, the understanding of the visual arts is still hindered by the literary aspirations and affections of art criticism, but if the art critics were to open their eyes, they would probably discover a new language: that of visuality.

In his article about *The Motif Notions of Elisabeth Frenzel and Raymond Trousson*, Alain Préaux points out that both scholars have gained international fame and importance as representatives of classic thematology. He attempts to represent the problematic nature of Frenzel's ever evolving motif notion. In passing, possible similarities between some of her ideas and the considerations of some members of the research group are highlighted.

Though Trousson's contribution to motivology has been fairly restricted, his definition is entered into first. In his opinion, the motif is the philosophical background ('backcloth') of a literary work. It may refer either to a certain basic attitude (e.g. revolt) or to an impersonal situation in which the characters are not yet individualized (e.g. the situation of the man between two women). In this sense, the motif may also exist outside literature. Frenzel, for her part, calls the basic attitude — such as revolt (or love) — theme, for it is a static concept which requires a further specification (e.g. «against the father») to fulfil the dynamic function which marks the motif.

Frenzel and Trousson differentiate methodogically between the study of motifs and the study of «matter». The poet who wants to use a certain matter is by definition dependent on the literary tradition that has been created by that matter. Therefore, every study of matter has to contain a detailed introduction concerning the history of the matter and its reception by the author studied (i.e. the so-called *Längsschnitt-Technik*). The author who treats a motif, on the other hand, may be far less dependent on the literary tradition, for the biographical, economical, political and social context may determine the emergence of or preference for a certain motif (here, the *Querschnitt-Technik* is appropriate).

Both Frenzel and Trousson advocate the «*Stoffgeschichte*» (history of matter). The problem, however, is how to define the notion «matter». Frenzel tries to do this by playing it off against the notions «theme» and «motif». She stresses the fact that a concatenation or a complex of motifs produce the «matter». In one of her later works she simply states that the «matter» is bound to established names and events.

In the meantime, she has become interested primarily in the motif. She defines the motif as an seminal constituent part of a matter which is primarily characterized by its capacity for combining with other motifs. As compared to the matter, the motif is a small, substantial unit which contains a situational element. But the motif may also be larger than the matter, for it expresses something general, unspecified and changeable as well. Its situational and figurative character distinguishes the motif from the more abstract, non-situational theme (or problem) and from smaller substantial components such as the topos and the image, which are purely figurative and decorative. In other words: the motif has to be pinned down between two poles: a spiritual one and a formal one. It is not purely spiritual, for it has an expressive character: neither is it purely expressive, for it has a spiritual tension by which it is distinguished from the current motif notion in the visual arts. What is called motif in the visual arts, is called «trait» in literary theory, according to Frenzel. There is a large gap between Frenzel's notion of the motif and that of art historians and musicologists. But Frenzel manages to bridge the gap between motif and trait. In her system, a trait may receive the value of a motif and a motif may be devalued to a trait.

Frenzel's definitions come very close to Hadermann's. With Hadermann, Frenzel regards the theme as a static invariant around which varying motifs rally. The motif may be characterized either by the contrast or analogy between two images or by a conflictive situation with on the one hand a concept and on the other hand an image which gives concrete form to this concept. Generally speaking, the tension marking the motif consists of two words which create a «situation», set the action going and bring as yet anonymous characters into conflict with each other.

The relation between motifs may be dependent on the literary genre in which they occur. The absolute domination of the basic motif is typical of drama. The epic, on the contrary, is marked by the coordination of numerous motifs. In fact, Frenzel's hierarchy of motifs is not a rigid system, since each substantial component may be devalued as well as revalued. Any element may therefore take the place of any other element in the hierarchy. Ornamental motifs may be completely eliminated but they may also acquire the value of a basic motif. Besides, an author who has often used a basic motif may parody and devalue it in the course of time, so that it reoccurs only as a side-motif. In her contribution (cfr. supra) Annie Philippot-Reniers has described such a devaluation in the visual arts. Alternatively, traits, images or topoi may be revalued and thus become motifs pushing along the action.

In her work Frenzel also mentions «type-motifs» by which she means characters who indicate a well-defined situation but do not have a proper name (e.g. the insurgent). According to Trousson, however, the type is not a motif, for it is a character and by no means a concept or a situation.

Alain Préaux concludes that Trousson has made a considerable contribution towards thematology by developing a terminology for the study of matter and type, but that with regard to the study of motifs, Frenzel's system is far more interesting. Her complex motif notion shows many points of resemblance to ideas that have been formulated in the visual arts. Therefore, her flexible system may exercise a stimulating influence on the interdisciplinary study of motifs.

In *The Notions «Matrix» and «Hypogram» in Riffaterre's Poetics*, David Gullentops presents a description of Riffaterre's poetic system as it has been put forward in *Semiotics of poetry* as well as an application of it to the poem «La Morte» by Emile Verhaeren.

According to Riffaterre, decoding a poem always starts with a first reading in which the reader tries to grasp the meaning. His linguistic competence allows him to discover incompatibilities between words, ungrammaticalities with regard to the representation of reality (mimesis), and through his literary competence he is forced to refer the sequence marked by those ungrammaticalities to a so-called «hypogram», i.e. «a system comprising at least a predication, and it may be as large as a text». In the course of the first reading, we pass beyond the level of meaning (mimesis) to arrive at the level of significance (semiosis). Once the ungrammaticalities have been tracked down they are assembled in a paradigm and become variants of the same structure: the matrix, i.e. «a minimal and literal sentence which transforms itself into a longer, complex and nonliteral periphrasis». This transformation comes about by two specific rules: expansion and conversion. These operations establish a continual relation between the matrix and the text which is derived from it. This relation constitues the text's significance and gives it a semantic unity.

In Verhaeren's poem, the 'cadavre de ma raison' floating in an English river, refers undoubtedly to Ophelia's death. Normally, the image of Ophelia's death evokes beauty and sweetness as well as a sense of pity, but in Verhaeren's poem the image carries above all a masochistic overtone. Love of death is changed into aversion to life. The negative connotations of the image cause the whole port of London to be described in a negative way according to the matrix. This offers a clear example of what Riffaterre would call conversion. The description of the cross-referring noises in the poem, on the other hand, constitues an example of expansion, although the forms in which they are expressed grow less complex in the course of the poem. We are in fact dealing with an expansion in the wrong direction, revealing Verhaeren's need always to explain his message, in this case the denial of life.

Remarkably, there are a lot of similarities between Riffaterre's system and Van Gorp's. Both attach much importance to semiotics (inter-textuality), stylistic criteria (ungrammaticalities) and to the idea that a text forms a semantic unity. Van Gorp also makes use of the notion «matrix», but here the difference between both theoreticians comes to the surface. Van Gorp compares his notion of «formal matrix» to Riffaterre's hypogram, but they do not altogether coincide. The hypo-gram is not a mere formal element but it guides the interpretation through transference from mimesis to semiosis.

The contribution by Léon Somville and Michel Pierrard dealing with *the ternary sentence in Paul Claudel's «Connaissance de l'Est»* is concerned with an analysis of a recurrent sentence structure in the prose poems of the above work. It is based on a corpus made up of 18 canonical sentences showing an identical ternary structure:
1) the initial sequence, which consists of one or more propositions and is followed by a punctuation mark (comma or semicolon);
2) the intercalated sequence, which is introduced by the conjunction 'et' and comprises at least one determiner of the final sequence;
3) the final sequence, which comprises at least the subject and the main verb of a non-subordinated proposition.

While repeated in a significant way, the stylistic mark becomes a motif. The particular organisation of a given utterance is not in the first place a matter of the writing of an author (tics, procedures etc), but it is first and foremost a product of the «imagination of the structure».

Claudel, however, was not the first to use the ternary sentence. It originated in the work of Chateaubriand and was perfected by Flaubert (*Madame Bovary*), but above all, Claudel was indebted to a contemporary of his, Jules Renard, who made use of the ternary structure as well. Here, therefore, we are dealing with a «hypogram», a motif which is liable to migrate from one literary genre to another, always in search of new semantic input.

To be complete, the analysis may not neglect the fact that the motif is a formal as well as a semantic unit. As a formal unit it reminds the readers of what they have read before, the *intertext*: as a semantic, signifying element it appears as an exemplary, explicit rendition of a *matrix* which is likely to generate the entire text.

Two elements are highly important in the syntactic description of the ternary model: the intercalated sequence and the conjunction 'et'. The structure of Claudel's ternary sentence differs considerably from the classic model ternary sentence as used by Chateaubriand and Flaubert. In the classic model the intercalated sequence was still part of the final sequence, but Claudel turned it into an autonomous constituent of the sentence. A close examination of the ternary sentences in *Connaisance de l'Est* reveals 6 intermediate steps towards an ever greater autonomy of the intercalated sequence. Several variants mark a similar progression towards autonomy on the part of the coordinating conjunction 'et'. That covers the analysis of the motif as a formal unit. There remains the analysis of the contents of the motif. Starting from an underlying semantic structure — the *matrix* in the Riffaterrean terminology — the poem tries to accomplish itself in language, but along itineraries of predilection, marked out for the reader's intention. In order to explain the sudden appearance of meaning in a certain type of discourse, one has to use the procedures which have been put to the test in semiotics.

According to semiotic theory, intercalation results in a temporal, spatial or rhetorical *shifting out*. 'Shifting out' means that the continuity of discourse is interrupted. Temporal shifting out, for instance, means that there is a hiatus in the temporal sequence of a given utterance. However, the distortions which are introduced by the intercalated sequence are situated merely on the level of appearance and they always end up by being neutralised on the level of being.

In semiotic terms, *neutralisation* mostly presents itself as the manifestation of the semantic axis instead of one of its terms. The matrix of *Connaissance de l'Est* reads as follows: «La mort, en Chine, tient autant de place que la vie». The ternary structure subordinates the contrast between life and death to an egalitarian logic («autant de place»). In the same way, the most fundamental semantic categories are lexicalised by means of antinomic pairs (culture/barbarism, animate/inanimate, exteroceptivity/interoceptivity). But the apparent oppositions are invariably neutralised, since the text actualises the chosen semantic category in its entirety. Each time, discourse expresses difference in order to signify harmony.

The ternary structure characteristically involves «*nesting*». This term designates the way in which one duration (either long or short), space or volume (whether restricted or not) fits into another space, duration or volume. Nesting is related to another remarkable feature of the ternary structure: its *iconicity*. By this is meant that the length of a piece of text reflects the duration of the action expressed by it. In Claudel, the subject of the action often occupies a nodal space at the end of his quest. Of this «nested» space the intercalation is the indicator and the image.

It appears that the ternary structure allows Claudel to actualise the additional meaning linked to the poetic function of language. However, the intercalation does not bring the matrix into discursive existence every time. It may also function as a rhetorical ornament which emphasises certain elements. This is not to say that this «*emphatisation*» may be considered as mere padding, for it marks an oscillation towards one of the poles of a unique structure: the constituent form-meaning of the ternary sentence motif.

In *From Scale to Circle and Kernel* Dina Van Berlaer-Hellemans examines the construction of a leitmotif and the clustering of leitmotifs in three novels by Jan Wolkers, viz. *De walgvolgel, De perzik van onsterfelijkheid* and *Brandende liefde*. In so doing, she tries to test the instruments offered by the research group for their practical value. As a touchstone, the motif of the Grail is chosen.

When taken as a motif transmitted by the cultural tradition — as is the case in Lampo's œuvre — the Grail is not very interesting since it is too easy to translate. Fortunately, Wolkers treated this motif in a more fascinating way.

De walgvogel contains quite a few «leitmotifs»: they are rapidly heralded and regularly repeated as in music, but they attain their full development ... as a motif. According to this pattern, the Grail is hastily introduced but then the reader starts to stumble over all too many pots, glasses, scales, bowls, jars etc. Subsequently, the Grail is connected with other leitmotifs. First of all with the girl, Lien, and with the eglantine, which is, according to the Rosicrucians, an equivalent of the Grail. The eglantine, in turn, is related to painting. This explains at once how hermetic motifs get into Wolkers' novels. The writer became acquainted with the hermetic cultural heritage through painting. In his novels, paintings often provide the link between realistic depiction and symbolic meaning. In addition there are also oriental motifs in *De walgvogel*, such as the mandala (circle) and the patra (Buddha's cosmic scale). In fact, we are facing a remarkable fusion of oriental and occidental motifs: rose and lotus, Grail and patra actually merge. The I-protagonist puts Lien (West) on a par with India (East), for both represent the goal of his quest. The joining of all these elements constitutes a dynamic process pushing the entire work to its global meaning. And, as was to be expected, all the above leitmotifs come together in the final scenes of the novel. The quest ends in suffering and death, without redemption, without a hereafter, resulting only in all-pervading emptiness. This corresponds to the eastern view, for the patra is said to contain a twofold emptiness.

The mandala-motif survived *De Walgvogel*. It reoccurs in *De perzik van onsterfelijkheid* where it helps to develop the dynamics of the narrative structure. Leitmotifs, however, are completely absent in this novel, but in *Brandende liefde*, the Grail again plays a structuring role. Represented by a ewer, it is immediately connected to the most important motif of this novel: the stone (the philosopher's stone was an equivalent of the Grail as far back as Wolfram). The stone, for its part, is associated with scales, circles (mandala), peach stones etc. At the end of the novel, the basic motif is transformed into the theme: the stone, being the essence of existence, stands for the inner rebirth which remains possible in spite of suffering and death.

Various conclusions may be drawn from this analysis. It stands out clearly that motifs may act as the motor of the narrative structure. Besides, static motifs may become dynamic and vice versa. And, as all kinds of accretions may occur, it is certainly not advisable to cut up the motif range unequivocally. In any case, the emergence, construction and evolution of recurrent motifs requires a thorough examination.

In Sven-Claude Bettinger's contribution *Movement and Movements: a Theme and its Motifs*, the results of Dina Van Berlaer-Hellemans' analysis (cfr. supra) are applied to two recent prose texts by Jürgen

Becker, an author who differs considerably from Wolkers in many respects.

Becker said of one of his first writings that it demonstrated the movement of a consciousness through reality and its transformation in language. He called his early writings «intermedial», by which he meant that the traditional genre distinctions were blurred so that the observing subject uttering its registrations, assessments and reflections became the most important point of reference.

In 1981, Becker's novel *Erzählen bis Ostende* was published. It offers a detailed description of a train journey from Cologne to Ostend. The story is not chronologically related, but it is continually interrupted by disparately mounted recollections and thoughts of the narrator. All kinds of events are recalled synchronically, but they have to be related diachronically. Logically and technically, the action takes place on more than one level. As a result, the story is full of complex rotary movements: words continually create the illusion of movement, much like Op-art. Such a writing technique is certainly not new. It had already been tried out by expressionists, dadaists and surrealists.

Gradually it becomes clear that the main character in the story, alias the narrator, makes the same sort of movements. He projects his past experiences into the future. When he catches sight of the sea in Ostend, he stills his inner unrest — or perhaps he does not, for «sea» is a word with a plural symbolic meaning. It may be associated with movement, but also with continuity and rest as its movements repeat themselves endlessly through the same pattern. The narrator's unrest reflects the indecision of the world surrounding him. An endless, almost unsolvable dialectic process governs the whole of society. It is like a never-ending film forever showing the same ever-recurring images and situations. From this perspective, the sea becomes an image of hope signifying movement, change, escape, infinity. In the narrator's eyes, it stands for the possibility of overcoming his personal crisis and that of the world around him.

Erzählen bis Ostende is related in more than one way to Becker's latest novel *Die Türe zum Meer*. Doors play an important role in both novels and both novels end in Ostend during an autumn storm. In *Die Türe zum Meer* hope has been mitigated. Snow has taken the place of the sea, the image of hope. Snow too is water, it is true, but it is water in an altered, semi-solid state, unstable, unreliable, transient and, above all, cold. The only place which has not yet been deformed by the omnipresent alienation is the garden, the 'hortulus animae' in which man can hide and live as an exile. In this way, escape is connected to captivity in a narrow space. Escape is no longer a real possibility, it has become fiction.

It clearly appears from Bettinger's analysis that movement is the theme of both novels. But at the end of a spiral, the movements eventually form a circle. Therefore, the same motifs keep recurring: the sea, the journey, the door, the land, the wind, the rain ... and also the snow. These motifs are almost freely interchangeable. In spite of all concrete descriptions, we do not know whether it is reality or fiction that we are escaping from or fleeing towards. This uncertainty, reflecting the social reality, requires a regular repetition of the same motifs. They offer at least some hold in the formal sense, for they give the text an organic, be it disorderly structure. All in all, it seems that the motif is, more so than the theme, a predominant feature of modern literature.

*
* *

The research findings described in the above paragraphs provide the framework within which the symposium *Motifs in Arts and Literature* should be situated: the team working on «Motievenstudie» wanted to hear the opinions of well-known foreign scholars on its research field. What they had to say about it is to be found in the following texts, where the point of view of literary theory and criticism is represented by Jean Burgos (Chambéry) and Margaret Davies (London), that of other arts by the musicologist Constantin Floros (Hamburg) and the film semiologist Eric De Cuyper (Nijmegen).

A general conclusion will not be attempted at the end of these pages: it is left to the reader, who will surely be able to discern agreements and disagreements on the principles of a possible interartistic motif research in the different papers presented.

Brussels, September 1986.
The Editors

Jean BURGOS
(Université de Chambéry)

LA NOTION DE MOTIF DANS LES RECHERCHES SUR L'IMAGINAIRE

En un temps où le sérieux fait d'assez grands ravages, il me semble nécessaire de considérer toute méthode critique, si séduisante soit-elle, d'un œil particulièrement ironique, sans prévention dévote, ni précipitation zélatrice, afin d'éviter d'adhérer «comme les huîtres et les sots», selon la belle formule de Valéry que depuis longtemps j'ai faite mienne.

Cette distance ironique, sans doute lieu commun dans son affirmation mais beaucoup moins commun dans son application, n'est en rien précaution oratoire qui devrait me permettre désormais de chevaucher allègrement, sans référence ni révérence d'aucune sorte. Elle n'est pas davantage alibi pour folâtrer à l'aventure, et peu sérieusement, dans les terres de l'Imaginaire où je vais devoir m'aventurer. Mais elle me paraît bien plutôt précaution indispensable, plus encore que partout ailleurs, en matière de recherche sur l'Imaginaire, c'est-à-dire en un domaine qui par définition ne se laisse pas clore, supporte mal les éclairages crus, se révèle dans des changements plus que dans des états, implique à coup sûr celui qui s'y risque, et qui finalement ne propose à l'analyse que des traces — ces fragiles images — sur des parcours à découvrir et dont la direction importe bien plus que le terme.

Dans ces conditions, comment ne pas redouter tout ce qui de quelque façon voudrait s'ériger en système et comment ne pas se méfier, sauf à vouloir en rire, de toute grille qu'il suffirait d'appliquer dès après lecture de son mode d'emploi, comme de toute formalisation prétendant enfermer dans des formules et diagrammes le monde même de l'ouverture et l'infini des possibles qui en procède? C'est par là déjà reconnaître que, à l'écart de toute chapelle, les quelques réflexions que voici, récusant les herméneutiques réductrices aussi bien que les phénoménologies pragmatistes, se proposent seulement de voir comment et dans quelles limites le motif peut être un outil utile, voire indispensable, dans l'exploration de l'Imaginaire du texte, que l'écriture de ce texte soit verbale, picturale, musicale ou autre. Ou plus précisément de voir si le motif, entre le thème trop substantiel et la structure trop purement formelle, ne pourrait pas servir à repérer les points d'ancrage des nœuds d'images sur les schèmes moteurs qui parcourent le texte comme aussi les modalités de tissage de ces schèmes qui déterminent les parcours obligés du texte, et par là contribuer efficacement à l'actualisation du texte, dans la lecture de son Imaginaire, par la réalisation des possibles qui l'habitent.

* *
*

Ce serait une folle gageure que de vouloir résumer en quelques mots les recherches actuelles sur l'Imaginaire, les moyens qu'elles se donnent, les fins qu'elles se proposent. Outre que ce serait caricaturer à l'extrême une démarche qui n'a cessé de s'affirmer au cours de ces dix dernières années après s'être longtemps cherchée et qui supporte mal les schématisations, cela risquerait fort de conduire à adapter la notion de motif à une méthode déjà en place, si tâtonnante soit-elle, quand il faudrait montrer au contraire comment cette notion se met effectivement au service d'une approche toujours à réinventer.

Pour situer le débat, je rappellerai seulement, au risque de me paraphraser, que l'Imaginaire, sur son versant qui nous importe ici, peut se définir comme ce carrefour où viennent converger d'une part les multiples pressions qui, du monde extérieur, viennent s'infléchir en nous, accommodant sans cesse notre moi au gré de forces qui nous contraignent à devenir ce que nous sommes, et d'autre part les pulsions profondes qui, émergeant à chaque instant, viennent remodeler le monde extérieur, l'assimilant et le corrigeant en fonction de ce moi en devenir. Ce carrefour d'échanges, où se joue ce qu'il y a en nous de plus vivant, la relation du moi du monde, c'est aussi celui où se situe l'écriture.

Au point de rencontre et d'échanges de forces antagonistes et complémentaires, les unes émanant du sujet écrivant, les autres du monde où il prend place, le texte, dans une telle perspective, ne saurait être considéré ni comme simple reflet d'un monde extérieur ni comme seul projet d'un monde profond, puisque de la rencontre de ces forces naît une réalité qui tient ses pouvoirs et son dynamisme des deux sources d'où elles surgissent, certes, mais ne saurait être réductible à aucune d'elles prise séparément. Cela signifie que si l'écriture, quelle que soit la forme qu'elle revêt, procède essentiellement d'un jeu de forces, son déchiffrement ne saurait aucunement se dissocier du déchiffrement de la résultante de ces forces se prolongeant et résonnant en une réalité langagière proprement poétique, c'est-à-dire neuve absolument.

Cette réalité neuve tient sans doute à l'organisation des matériaux en place — les images ou plutôt leurs traces — au gré de métamorphoses successives appelant, et même incluant, jusqu'aux ruptures génératrices de formes nouvelles qu'elles suscitent. Mais elle tient davantage encore, cette réalité, aux modalités de fonctionnement de ce tissu vivant qu'est le texte se tissant lui-même selon certains itinéraires obligés, ces schèmes moteurs sur lesquels viennent se greffer dans leurs métamorphoses les matériaux de tous ordres et dont la convergence détermine le sens à venir.

C'est dire déjà, sans entrer plus avant dans le détail, que dans une telle optique la lecture du texte — et pas seulement du texte verbal, que cela soit clair — est inséparable de la prise en charge des forces qui le sous-tendent et qu'il convient de réactiver.

*
*   *

Si donc l'écriture de l'Imaginaire peut se définir, du fait de ses sources, comme une organisation de matériaux répondant à des modalités qui lui sont propres et trouvant sens dans les finalités mêmes qu'elle poursuit, la lecture de l'Imaginaire, elle, va consister à déceler les forces orientées qui habitent le texte, à les suivre dans leurs déroulements et leurs intrications, à les actualiser jusqu'à faire de l'œuvre non plus un document ni un simple objet d'étude mais bien un organisme vivant qu'il convient d'appréhender comme tel.

Or, les difficultés ne manquent pas dans pareille entreprise qui exige une paradoxale attitude de sympathie et d'ironie conjointes, mais implique surtout que ne soit jamais perdue de vue la double fonction référentielle et génératrice des matériaux en présence. C'est là que nous rencontrons une première fois le motif, lequel pourrait d'abord se définir comme un regroupement isomorphe et récurrent de matériaux à valeur à la fois sémiotique et symbolique et susceptible de manifester, à l'intérieur d'un même texte et mieux encore d'une même œuvre, la fonction à la fois signifiante et productive d'une écriture.

Si en effet le déchiffrement de l'écriture de l'Imaginaire implique que soient pris en considération non pas quelques éléments du texte que l'on pourrait croire exemplaires — ceux que pendant longtemps on a voulu nommer images et sur lesquels les manuels en usage dans les classes se plaisent encore malencontreusement à attirer l'attention — mais bien tous les matériaux sans exception aucune, il apparaît urgent de ne plus distinguer ceux qui relèveraient de la seule analyse formelle portant sur les signifiants en action et ceux qui relèveraient d'une analyse thématique s'attachant aux valeurs symboliques des signifiés. Or le motif, justement, par les variations qu'il entraîne et provoque tout en soulignant, par ses reprises mêmes, la permanence du trajet directeur sous la diversité des apparences, ne nous rappelle-t-il pas, si nous devions l'oublier, qu'on ne saurait séparer la fonction génératrice des matériaux d'un langage s'organisant en écriture, dans un champ sémantique déterminé, de leur fonction référentielle qui leur assure leur concrétude mais aussi le dynamisme qui les nourrit?

* * *

Mais il y a plus. Le déchiffrement de l'écriture de l'Imaginaire, la mise au jour de ses lignes de force, implique en effet que puissent être décelés les processus de métamorphose des matériaux en présence et qui vont donner pouvoir à ces matériaux de faire image en se regroupant et se déformant progressivement. Voilà qui n'est guère facile dès lors surtout que l'on constate que ces regroupements er déformations ne s'opèrent pas à l'intérieur de structures préexistantes mais qu'elles sont elles-mêmes modes de structuration d'un langage qui se plie à leurs contraintes et s'oriente selon les forces qu'ils recèlent et transmettent, à tous leurs niveaux et dans toutes leurs manifestations — rythmiques, phoniques, sémantiques, rhétoriques ou autres. Constater cela c'est constater que l'image ne saurait être contenue toute entière dans un phonème ou un mot mais qu'elle est indissociable d'une syntaxe qui fait partie de sa nature autant que de sa fonction; c'est constater donc qu'il ne saurait y avoir d'archétypes substantifs, comme d'aucuns le voudraient, susceptibles de déterminer une typologie de l'Imaginaire. Mais c'est constater aussi que les modes d'articulation entre les matériaux faisant image et les modalités de fonctionnement qui en découlent seuls peuvent aider à déceler les processus de l'Imaginaire en acte dans une écriture.

Il apparaît déjà par là que le motif qui nous importe ici — dans la mesure où il est plus précisément organisation structurée et structurante de matériaux dont l'unité, et donc le caractère non aléatoire bien manifesté par sa récurrence, s'impose d'elle-même — le motif se montre d'une utilité primordiale pour le déchiffrement d'une écriture de l'Imaginaire. En effet, non seulement il fait fonction de révélateur d'une réalité échappant au discours et ne renvoyant à aucune détermination logique préétablie (ce qui serait le cas du simple motif ornemental qui n'est jamais que stéréotype), mais il permet de mettre particulièrement en relief, de par la permanence des rapports qu'il maintient entre des matériaux qui ne cessent pour leur part de se déformer, tout à la fois la singularité d'une écriture et son authenticité.

Est-ce à dire que le motif, assurant et tout en même temps révélant des groupements caractéristiques et réitératifs de matériaux prenant signification exemplaire, hors de leurs dénotations propres, dans leurs regroupements mêmes et par eux, puisse tout au plus alerter sur certaines particularités d'un texte ou d'un ensemble de textes et manifester au mieux l'originalité d'une œuvre, au pire les tics de son créateur? Il en serait ainsi si nous devions nous contenter, dans l'analyse d'une écriture en ses cheminements créatifs, de déceler des constellations d'images qui seraient autant de nébuleuses ayant pour noyau quelque archétype substantif tout droit sorti du catalogue de la manufacture des armes et cycles de l'inconscient. Si c'est ainsi bien souvent, hélas, qu'ont tourné court les recherches sur l'Imaginaire, celles du moins qui se contentaient d'explorer de façon bien hasardeuse et plus encore stérile les conditionnements pesant sur l'œuvre entendue comme produit fini, et bien fini, en revanche des recherches plus récentes ne s'en tiennent pas là qui s'attachent à l'ensemble des possibles libérés par l'œuvre entendue comme production et point de départ d'une création toujours continuée. Aux constellations d'images et au ciel fixe qu'elles proposent, ces recherches entendent substituer des réseaux dont les matériaux, de par les forces qu'ils échangent et les structures d'équilibre qui en résultent, font image; mais elles entendent plus encore s'attacher à déceler la façon dont ces réseaux, véritables nœuds de l'Imaginaire, se greffent et reprennent vie sur les grands schèmes moteurs qui parcourent le texte et lui donnent statut de vivant.

La mise au jour de réseaux privilégiés tendant à se répéter sous des formes sensiblement similaires et dotés de valeurs symboliques analogues mais fonctionnant à des niveaux différents (réseaux qui sont des structures pleines trouvant signification dans leur fonctionnement même) pourrait bien dès lors nous aider à définir le motif de façon plus pertinente encore. Mais cette mise au jour devrait surtout nous inciter à voir dans ce motif non pas une structure latente susceptible de révéler, en tant que marque stylistique, l'appartenance à quelque discours sous-jacent tendant à se manifester, mais bien au contraire une structure manifeste échappant à toute intentionnalité d'un discours autre et participant à l'émergence progressive d'une réalité contemporaine de son énonciation.

* * *

C'est par là, sans doute, que le motif va se révéler le plus fructueux dans l'exploration d'une écriture de l'Imaginaire qui s'attache à voir comment les réseaux de matériaux qui font image, ces nœuds de l'Imaginaire, en s'inscrivant précisément sur les schèmes qui animent et orientent le texte, vont engendrer une syntaxe nouvelle, à l'écart des sentiers du discours, syntaxe qui seule laisse le texte parler en son nom propre. Car s'il est vrai que tous les matériaux sont à prendre à considération dans une telle exploration, dès lors surtout qu'ils s'organisent en réseaux, tous ces réseaux cependant ne revêtent pas les caractères du motif, et par cela d'abord qu'ils ne sont qu'exceptionnellement isomorphes et encore plus rarement récurrents; il n'en reste pas moins que l'examen des motifs comme réseaux imagés privilégiés se montre d'un intérêt extrême dès lors que l'on s'attarde sur leurs modalités d'ancrage dans le texte.

Il se pourrait en effet que la récurrence du motif, en dépit bien souvent des apparences, tînt moins à la reproduction pure et simple des éléments qui le composent — lesquels au contraire semblent continuellement se déformer, nous l'avons vu, au sein d'une structure dont l'isomorphie est garantie essentiellement par des rapports de forces — qu'à ses modalités d'insertion régulière sur les grands schèmes moteurs qui l'appellent comme manifestation concrète et urgente dont ils ont besoin pour se manifester et se régénérer tout à la fois. Dans une telle perspective, il apparaît que la reprise du motif en ses multiples variations n'assure pas à l'œuvre, comme on pourrait le croire d'abord, une continuité significative qui serait garante de son unité, mais qu'elle est tout à l'inverse la preuve concrète et rassurante, toujours redonnée, d'une unité dictée par la convergence des schèmes moteurs et dont la cohérence détermine le sens même de l'œuvre.

Ces schèmes, qui d'une certaine façon constituent en effet l'ossature du texte, occupent une place importante dans le déchiffrement d'une écriture de l'Imaginaire. Les déceler, c'est à la fois découvrir le canevas de ce texte et se mettre en mesure d'en saisir l'unité, de la faire revivre. Il semble bien dès lors que ce soit par eux que s'opère le passage de l'écriture à la lecture de l'Imaginaire. Parce qu'ils catalysent les réseaux de matériaux qui font image, parce qu'ils les orientent dans leurs métamorphoses mais imposent aussi, dans ce passage à la différence sans lequel il n'y aurait pas création, certains rappels et certaines reprises qui garantissent l'identité au sein même de cette différence, les schèmes pourraient être les meilleurs pourvoyeurs des motifs; en tout cas eux seuls, dans cet univers bien peu raisonnable où j'ai choisi d'avancer, peuvent en rendre raison.

*
* *

Le motif cependant n'est-il que ce garde-fou rassurant répétant la permanence du même sous la diversité de l'autre, voire la permanence de certaine réalité sous la diversité du paraître langagier? Certainement pas si nous examinons ses diverses fonctions qui font de lui, dans le champ d'intervention qui est nôtre, bien autre chose que l'occasion de repérer des séries où se reproduisent des mots-clefs dignes on ne saurait trop pourquoi d'être applaudis, ou l'occasion de surprendre par les trous de serrure du texte les tares secrètes d'un acteur mis à nu. Car dans la mesure où, par sa récurrence et son isomorphisme apparent, mais aussi par son symbolisme persévérant, il attire l'attention sur les schèmes qui l'appellent et qu'il nourrit, le motif cesse bientôt de n'être qu'un outil dans l'approche de l'écriture de l'Imaginaire pour devenir instrument de lecture et d'une lecture vivante qui est rencontre de l'Imaginaire refroidi dans le texte et de l'Imaginaire du lecteur réveillé à son contact. Aussi bien, et d'abord parce qu'il ne passe pas inaperçu et se fait d'autant plus remarquer qu'il a été repéré une première fois, mais aussi parce que son double aspect structurant et structuré, fascinant, entraîne à l'adopter, ce motif va-t-il à sa façon contraindre à découvrir une ligne de lecture s'inventant et se précisant à mesure, ou plutôt un sens de lecture, aussitôt que perçu le schème qu'il incarne. Il va contraindre à mener une lecture toujours plus avant, une lecture jalonnée par ses reprises dictant le rythme du texte aussi bien que ses carrefours, soulignant les divers itinéraires sans exclure aucun des possibles, explorant le présent et renvoyant ailleurs, manifestant et produisant du sens à la fois, et finalement aidant à saisir l'unité de l'œuvre en ses cheminements multiples et donc à l'actualiser.

* *
*

Quelque grande que soit l'utilité de cet outil-motif dans l'exploration de l'Imaginaire du texte, celui-ci fût-il graphique, pictural, musical, cinématographique, architectural aussi bien que verbal, il convient toutefois d'en mesurer les limites. Ces limites, me semble-t-il, se découvrent d'abord dans le fait que si le motif est d'une utilité peu discutable au niveau du déchiffrement d'une écriture, dans la mesure où il est une structure pleine où mouvements et matériaux s'informent mutuellement, s'il engage donc à refuser avant toute chose la dichotomie entre la forme et la matière qu'entretiennent et souvent malgré eux tant les thématiciens que les structuralistes de pure obédience, il risque bien cependant d'apparaître un peu encombrant dès lors que la lecture du texte refuse de

déboucher sur une interprétation quelle qu'elle soit et refuse aussi de
chercher sa fin dans le texte lui-même, mais se propose au contraire
d'ouvrir sur un sens toujours à venir et qui ne saurait être jamais cerné.
Une lecture guidée par quelque herméneutique, quand bien même
prudente elle se méfie de toute mise à plat relevant de l'explication, ne
tarde pas en effet à privilégier dans le motif ses seuls contenus et à tirer
conclusions de leurs qualités particulières renvoyant à une réalité autre
que le texte interpréterait à sa façon. Inversement, une lecture s'attachant
aux seuls pouvoirs et prodiges du langage va reléguer à l'arrière-plan ces
contenus pour ne garder du motif que son caractère expressif, hors de
toute réalité autre que linguistique, et trouvant source et justification en
lui-même seulement, dans ce vase clos où le texte ne cesse de se
contempler et de refléter, les répétant, ses propres simulacres. Dans une
lecture de l'Imaginaire qui ne privilégie, elle, ni les seuls contenus, ni la
seule expression, mais accorde tous pouvoirs au langage — et d'abord
celui de réaliser des possibles, d'ajouter à la réalité en place un surcroît de
réalité — en raison de la double réalité dont il procède et qui lui assure à
la fois son dynamisme et son authenticité, dans une telle lecture le motif
devrait certes occuper une place capitale : sa double fonction intrinsèque
et extrinsèque pourrait enfin, semble-t-il, être pleinement mise à profit.
Ce n'est pourtant pas tout à fait le cas. Sans doute faudrait-il avoir le
temps de le montrer in concreto à partir d'un poème (je pense à
Michaux[1]), d'un tableau (je pense à Kandinsky[2]) ou d'un concerto (je
pense à Bartok[3]); car tout se passe comme si le motif, fondamental
pourtant dans l'organisation de ces trois écritures, devenait gênant ou du
moins opposait certaine résistance à sa remise en route dans la lecture.
Est-ce parce que son trop plein de signification expressive et productive,
dans le texte et au-delà du texte, empêche qu'un autre Imaginaire ne s'en
empare? Est-ce parce que sa récurrence et son isomorphisme, venant
sinon à faire oublier du moins à passablement estomper la nouveauté
apportée par chacune de ses manifestations, font douter de son authenticité et peut-être même de son dynamisme jusqu'à la présenter comme un
stéréotype? Est-ce parce que la tentation est grande, celle même de la
facilité à laquelle il est si agréable de succomber, de ne plus en faire qu'un
refrain ou le signe d'une obsession, selon que l'on n'arrive plus à y lire
qu'une tournure insistante ou qu'un symptôme inquiétant? Toujours est-

---

[1] « Paix dans les brisements » (Moments).
[2] Trente.
[3] Concerto pour orchestre.

il que le motif, qui si bien se décrit, se laisse parfois assez mal prendre en compte au point de dévier la lecture vers les seuls effets du texte, entendu comme produit linguistique, ou vers la seule interprétation du texte, entendu comme production d'un psychisme et d'un milieu.

* *
*

Mais il est une autre limite que je donnerais volontiers au motif, dans l'exploration de l'Imaginaire d'un texte qui nous importe ici, même si je suis conscient, en fixant cette limite, du caractère subjectif que je donne à la notion de motif. C'est celle, majeure à mes yeux, qui tient au fait que le motif, tel du moins que j'ai tenté de le cerner selon ses différents critères et à ses différents niveaux, pourrait bien ne pas trouver la même place, jouer les mêmes fonctions, et pour tout dire revêtir la même importance dans toutes les écritures. J'irai plus loin encore en avançant que, si le motif est caractéristique de certains régimes de l'Imaginaire, jusqu'à devenir mode d'identification et donc clé de lecture de certaines écritures, en revanche, quand bien même il ne cesserait de maintenir la continuité et l'unité du texte au travers des images et réseaux d'images qui opèrent leurs variations à partir et autour de lui, le motif est d'importance toute relative, voire négligeable, d'un certain point de vue, dans d'autres régimes de l'écriture de l'Imaginaire.

Il est vrai, sans doute, que nombre de réseaux qui font image tendent à réapparaître effectivement dans des structures formelles analogues et avec des fonctions symboliques similaires d'un texte à l'autre, d'une œuvre à l'autre. Il s'en faut de beaucoup toutefois que l'on soit en droit pour autant de parler de motif, à moins que de donner à cette notion telle extension qu'elle perde l'essentiel de sa compréhension au point que tout ce qui se répète de telle ou d'autre sorte puisse être nommé motif. Et je me garderai de confondre, en ce qui me concerne, le simple retour d'images, de groupement d'images ou de thèmes au sens musical du terme, avec le motif proprement dit qui implique non seulement une structure et un contenu, mais aussi une articulation avec un ou plusieurs schèmes moteurs lui assurant son dynamisme et lui permettant de fonctionner dans un certain sens, c'est-à-dire lui permettant de ne pas s'enfermer dans un perpétuel ressassement. Ainsi strictement défini, dans la perspective de recherches sur l'Imaginaire en action dans un texte, le motif ne va jouer un rôle d'importance que lorsqu'il permettra effectivement de repérer la façon dont les schèmes s'orientent et se croisent, tissent progressivement le texte, s'infléchissent ou se ramifient, s'estompent et réapparaissent, manifestant par là et conjointement l'organisation présente du texte et sa destination véritable. Or, il n'est guère qu'un type de syntaxe de l'Imaginaire, telle que j'ai pu la définir par ailleurs, qu'une modalité de structuration dynamique de l'écriture de l'Imaginaire qui véritablement donne toute priorité à cette articulation du motif avec les schèmes : c'est la structuration de repli qui correspond à une tendance profonde de refus du temps chronologique, et où l'angoisse devant la finitude est cherchée dans la délimitation d'espaces privilégiés où se mettre à l'abri du temps. Délimiter un espace dans le texte, un espace dans cet espace, un nouvel espace mieux protégé et plus réduit encore dans celui-ci, c'est faire en sorte de ne plus laisser pénétrer le temps. L'écriture du refus, qui est aussi écriture du refuge, apparaît ainsi comme une écriture cherchant à évacuer le temps par l'occupation d'espaces sans cesse réaménagés et de plus en plus miniaturisés ; une écriture qui se fonde d'abord sur les matériaux concrets les plus propres à protéger et renforcer ces refuges, et qui de ce fait utilise au mieux l'image dans sa matérialité comme dans sa fonction symbolique — l'absent auquel renvoie le présent de la chose étant perçu comme espace plus sûr à l'abri définitivement de toute intrusion extérieure, de toute intempérie temporelle. Une telle écriture, qu'il ne saurait être question d'analyser ici dans tous les méandres qu'elle s'invente ni dans toutes les figurations qu'elle emprunte, s'organise autour de grands schèmes qui sont de progression continue (pénétration et enfoncement), de restriction spatiale (enfermement, redoublement, emboîtement), de minimisation (miniaturisation), d'atténuation (conciliation, communion, fusion). Dans une telle écriture, où les articulations, se multipliant, vont tendre à rassembler, à rapprocher, à réunir les matériaux en présence jusqu'à les confondre, les relations causales et consécutives disparaissent au profit de relations de similitude qui tendent à minimiser les différences, à réduire les écarts, à estomper les frontières. Et pareillement, jamais autant que dans une telle écriture les images contradictoires ne vont si bien se renverser, échanger leurs pouvoirs réciproques, jamais surtout les reprises et répétitions ne vont prendre si grande importance, tant dans la multiplication des processus d'emboîtement et de mise en abyme que dans la réitération des réseaux et des matériaux isolés ayant valeur incantatoire. Voilà sans doute qui est bien rapide et schématique, mais — puisque tous les critères définissant le motif tant du point de vue des contenus que du point de vue de l'expression s'y trouvent réunis et pleinement mis à profit — cela devrait permettre pourtant de comprendre pourquoi dans le cas privilégié de cette écriture du refus, qui relève d'une syntaxe de l'euphémisme, le motif revêt une importance qu'il ne saurait revêtir dans aucun autre type d'écriture de l'Imaginaire ; importance capitale puisque tout à la fois il sert d'indice majeur dans l'identification de cette écriture et permet d'en suivre plus aisément les itinéraires comme d'en actualiser les desseins par la lecture.

*
* *

Ce ne sont là sans doute, et j'en suis bien conscient, que quelques réflexions sur la notion de motif et son utilisation dans les recherches sur l'Imaginaire. Réflexions fort incomplètes, au demeurant, et qui demanderaient pour prendre consistance, dépassant les généralités, de s'appuyer sur chacun des processus en action dans le déchiffrement de l'écriture de l'Imaginaire et dans la remise en route, en œuvre, de ses possibles. Mais réflexions surtout qui demanderaient d'être mises à l'épreuve de la réalité du texte, d'être éprouvées dans des œuvres et de faire vraiment leurs preuves.

Faute d'avoir pu être plus précis et plus concret — d'autres après moi, je ne saurais en douter, viendront combler ces manques — du moins puis-je espérer avoir montré que le motif qui nous rassemble ici n'est ni raison (le motif invoqué) ni sujet (le motif développé), ces deux acceptions majeures du terme dans la langue française et qui renvoient chacune, par un comble d'ironie qui n'est pas fait pour me déplaire, à l'un des niveaux d'analyse du motif tel que nous l'entendons, celui des contenus et celui de l'expression. Car c'est bien conjointement l'un et l'autre que se découvre le motif, dans les recherches sur l'Imaginaire : une structure pleine et orientée dont les matériaux et les mouvements ne cessent de s'informer les uns les autres, maintenant l'identité au sein de la différence et jouant bien, par là même, du double principe formateur et informateur, continu et discontinu, qui régit toute écriture de l'Imaginaire et plus largement toute poétique. Que la création s'y retrouve à ce compte, voilà qui vaut bien un colloque.

Léon SOMVILLE

(Vrije Universiteit Brussel)

VERS UNE SÉMANTIQUE DE L'IMAGE.

En proposant une *Poétique de l'Imaginaire* (Seuil, 1982) qui soit d'abord une «pratique» des modes d'organisation de l'image dans les textes réputés littéraires, Jean Burgos a voulu se démarquer d'entreprises récentes, placées sous l'égide de la linguistique, pour lesquelles la saisie des contenus le cède définitivement à l'analyse des formes.

Le mérite, en pareille occurrence, est d'éviter le retour pur et simple à Bachelard. C'est pourquoi l'auteur commence par établir le bilan des recherches qui ont contribué, dans des domaines aussi variés que la psychologie (C.G. Jung), l'épistémologie (J. Piaget). l'anthropologie (G. Durand), l'herméneutique (P. Ricœur) ou l'étude des mythes (M. Eliade, J. Rudhardt), à revaloriser la fonction symbolique comme à systématiser ses types d'intervention dans les conduites humaines ou les productions de l'esprit. De cette enquête, qui le passionne très visiblement, Jean Burgos retient surtout, nous semble-t-il, (a) la classification des «schèmes» (attitudes ou comportements archétypaux de l'espèce toujours susceptibles de provoquer des «représentations concrètes précises») telle que l'a établie G. Durand dans ses *Structures anthropologiques de l'Imaginaire* (P.U.F., 1963); (b) la leçon toute décisive de Jung, pour qui l'image ne peut être la *somme* de deux apports, l'un conscient, l'autre inconscient, mais leur *produit*; (c) le renversement de perspective proposé par Piaget et en vertu duquel «toute science n'est pas nécessairement causale». Mentionnons encore les travaux d'un René Thom, dont la théorie dite des «catastrophes» devrait rendre compte des relations conflictuelles entre schèmes d'un même texte.

La spécificité de la poétique au regard des autres sciences humaines pourrait sembler difficile à définir: c'est là l'enjeu de toute lecture, qui, pour être informée, doit «sortir» du texte qu'elle a commencé d'aborder. Jean Burgos, aussi bien, ne cesse d'insister sur la priorité à accorder au «tissage» des images dans l'espace délimité par le texte. Le choix est ici entre une archéologie (celle où se complaisait Bachelard) et une épiphanie: même si l'image a toujours des antécédents *organiques* et gravite autour de *schèmes* traduisant les attitudes fondamentales (révolte, refus, ruse) de l'homme en proie à l'angoisse d'*être-au-monde*, elle n'intéresse précisément le poéticien qu'au moment où elle s'inscrit dans une «syntaxe» (comprenons par là un arrangement verbal, une œuvre de langage), qu'au moment où elle se soumet à une structuration (régimes de l'antithèse et de l'euphémisme, régime dialectique) comme à certaines contraintes thématiques, stylistiques ou logiques propres à chacun de ces régimes.

La distinction ainsi proposée entre une *écriture* qui se ressent de ses origines partiellement inconscientes et une *lecture* dont la seule garantie est de retrouver les lignes de force organisant les constellations d'images, entre le *réel* du texte et son *devenir* possible, entre *motivation* et *sens*, pareille distinction prouve sa valeur opératoire dans la seconde partie de l'ouvrage de Jean Burgos : Michaux, Apollinaire, Saint-Pol Roux, Eluard et Saint-John Perse y font l'objet d'une analyse conforme aux postulats établis en un premier temps.

Le poéticien, à tout prendre, s'est-il si fort distingué de Bachelard ? A-t-on changé la finalité de la lecture «heureuse» : le *retentissement* de l'image, l'appréhension d'un sens symbolique à travers (et seulement à travers) une représentation concrète ? Nous ne croyons pas, sauf qu'à l'impressionnisme du vieux maître s'est substituée une démarche qui, véritable gageure à notre époque, passe sans heurt des présupposés théoriques à la pratique du texte.

Margaret DAVIES

(University of Reading)

VARIATIONS SINGULAR AND PLURAL

In *Avenir de la poésie* of 1937 Eluard gives voice to what I shall be taking as my particular theme: «Il nous faut peu de mots pour exprimer l'essentiel; il nous faut tous les mots pour le rendre réel.»[1] This remark highlights a crucial and most fruitful opposition: on the one hand, the unity, simplicity, indeed even bareness of what we are used to call the theme, on the other the multiplicity and diversity of the forms in which it decks itself out. A valid thematic criticism must surely concern itself not merely with penetrating through to the obsessional core — further that way of course lies psycho-analysis — not only with uncovering the lines of force of the imagination, however brilliantly that may be done; but also with the contemplation of the multiform disguises and surprises of its overt and concrete 'reality' (to use Eluard's term). To my mind it is in the inventiveness of these variations, in the constantly shifting interplay of their diversity within the unity of the basic theme, that the sheer joy of creativity, the poet's own, but also that which he excites in us the reader, most triumphantly expresses itself.

The opposition of the theme and variations is of course familiar enough. But where is it appropriate to situate the word "motif", which after all I have personally chosen to juxtapose with the word "variations" in my title? Are these terms in fact interchangeable as sometimes they appear to be? I fear that here one could spend a long time in arguing about definitions and splitting hairs of every hue. I hope that it will suffice here for me to indicate my own interpretation of the word.

I have come to it first by considering its etymology — from the vulgar Latin "motivus", a word which essentially conveys the idea of "movement". And it is this idea which I shall want to stress, in terms of the generating power of the motif, its use as a propelling force which sets the poem in motion. In this context certain remarks made with his customary brilliance and percipience by Julien Gracq have helped me in making a closer formulation. Focussing on this dynamic quality, but still applying it to theme, the "essential heart of the matter", he says in

---

[1] Paul Eluard: *Œuvres complètes*, Tome I, Pléïade, 1968, p. 526.

Préférences: "Je crois que les grands thèmes imaginatifs sont avant tout moteurs, sont des mouvements simples presque des gestes d'acceptation, de refus, de possession, d'évasion — les mêmes mouvements instinctifs au fond qui ordonnent la ligne de votre vie."[2] Later, however, still stressing the idea of movement, he uses the word "motif" and indeed isolates it between inverted commas. It is in fact one of the ways in which that basic essential movement or gesture expresses itself, its material, concrete manifestation. Here he explains that "l'image du départ — de l'instance de départ — traduit à sa manière un certain goût de dédoublement que je ne nie pas (il doit être commun à beaucoup de gens qui écrivent)".[3] It is the "goût du dédoublement" which is the basic theme, the image of departure of the motif. He then goes on to give another example which he actually calls the "motif" in inverted commas: "motif qui pourrait traduire le même mouvement d'une autre manière: l'idée d'être transporté sur un lieu élevé."

In then establishing the motif as one of the manifestations of the essential theme in concrete artistic terms, (in Gracq's case the topos of the high place) I am also led to reflect on another factor: that the word tends to have been used much more commonly in music and in painting than in literature: and that perhaps it is no coincidence that I am using it here in relation to poetry. For poetry, like music and like painting, is concerned to exploit the concrete aspect of its basic material, i.e. to use words in all the aspects of their "reality", their materiality as well as their abstract powers of signifying.

Looked at in this light, it is hardly surprising that a motif in poetry, like a visual motif in painting or in architecture, should be used decoratively as a figure which recurs within an overall pattern. (And indeed used in this way, the motif is itself a figure, a synecdoche of the general "essential" theme). So the motif can be seen then as a figure or image or image cluster, generating its associations which go to make up the pattern of the whole. But there is also another very important aspect of the poetic motif: namely the musical sense of a certain sequence of sounds, which spins out into a series of variations that explore new permutations, while still being held in indissoluble relationship to the central phonic core.

It would seem now a logical step to try to identify what I have called the central generating motif of the poem. I can of course do this only in

---

[2] Julien Gracq: *Préférences*, Corti, 1961, p. 62.
[3] *ibid.*, p. 63

the guise of a hypothesis. Many poets, too many in fact for this to be a mere coincidence, speak of the first line of a poem as something which is given, which comes to them unbidden, and more often than not as a certain musical pattern even before the actual words take shape or make sense. Valéry talks of this at length[4], Apollinaire would hum a tune until words accumulated round it[5], and he and Rimbaud significantly needed the physical rhythmical movement of walking to set the poetic mechanism going[6].

Without wanting here to delve into the whole mysterious question of poetic creation, but simply as one way of approaching the problem of the relationship of motif and variations in poetry, I should like to base my analysis on the following hypothesis that it is often the first line of a poem in *all* the aspects of its concrete reality, — its overall rhythm, its harmonic pattern, its individual sounds, as well as its abstract "meaning" and more concrete associations, which serves as the "point de départ", the trigger that sets the poem in motion, the fulcrum around which it gravitates. It is certainly for the reader the signal that first beckons to him as it were, attracting his ear and eye as well as his mind, and alerting him to the possibilities hidden within it for future development. These are then enjoyed because they are both similar to that initial motif and yet surprisingly other: they constantly relate back and yet, as constantly are in a state of becoming, which the final lines resolve in temporary harmony. It is also that initial motif which has triggered off the creation of the poem, that is most likely to stay in the reader's mind and eventually set into motion the mnenonic processes which will then recreate the poem. As I see it, it is then this essentially dynamic process which for both poet and reader is coiled within the tight spring of the first-line motif.

It will be clear that I have found this to be particularly apposite in the poetry of Paul Eluard. Perhaps I should justify my choice a little further. There are several reasons even apart from personal taste. First the undoubtedly musical quality of his poetry, and his interest in the visual arts and personal affinity with many painters, give me an obvious opportunity to stress the resemblances I have noted with the sister arts. But also, as my initial quotation makes evident, the essential messages

[4] cf. in particular *Mémoires du Poète*, Œuvres I, Pléïade, 1957, p. 1473-1476.

[5] cf. Marie-Jeanne Durry: 'Un secret d'Apollinaire' in *Le Flâneur des Deux Rives*, n°. 4, décembre 1954.

[6] cf. Jacques Plessen: *Promenade et Poésie. L'expérience de la marche et du mouvement dans l'œuvre de Rimbaud*, La Haye/Paris 1967.

come out loud and clear, the basic themes are simple and tirelessly repeated, the lines of force of his imagination seem clear-cut. On the one hand are the elements of "le bien" which gravitate round the central point of a shared love opening out to fuse with the natural world and thence with a love of humanity. On the other, "le mal" is constituted by absence which lead to an alienation from the natural world and humanity generally. However, throughout there is a constant dialectical movement which guides the poet through oppositions and tensions, to encompass the bad as a necessary component in a constant and dynamic process of being: "Ma pensée soutenue par la vie et la mort". And yet, and yet ...... poetry when it becomes predictable, ceases to be. It lives by the way it transforms the same into the other. Despite its clear-cut overall themes, the beauty and mystery of Eluard's poetry lie not only in its symmetry and regularity but also in the complex multiplicity of its variations. I have already stressed his preoccupation with making the essential real. But he is concerned not only with rendering account of "le réel" ("je rends compte du réel")[7]; even more than that, he declares "je comble le réel." And it is this over-filling, the spilling over of permutations and variations, and the ensuing surprising interplay between monolithic constant and organic, dynamic, decorative development that, to my mind, lie the succulence and beauty of his poetry.

I now propose to look more closely at some of his poems, paying particular attention to the ways in which the motif of the first line generates the ensuing structure. I have first chosen a poem which treats the essential theme of the effects of love in its good and positive aspects: "La courbe de tes yeux fait le tour de mon cœur." I then propose to take two poems which actually share the same first line."L'oreille du taureau à la fenêtre" is a pictorial motif, if not exactly taken from any one Picasso painting, at least inspired by the artist's treatment of the bull figure generally. Even within that clear frame of reference that identical motif will generate some very different connotations, and even manage to span across two distinct if not entirely opposing themes.

La courbe de tes yeux fait le tour de mon cœur.

Baudelaire of course is the real "magicien ès lettres," who announces his entrée en scène with veritable spells. "J'ai plus de souvenirs que si j'avais mille ans."[8] "O mère des souvenirs maîtresse des maîtresses."[9]

---

[7] In 'Poésie Ininterrompue', *Œuvres complètes*, Tome II, Pléiade, p. 30.

[8] Charles Baudelaire 'Spleen', Œuvres I, Pléïade, 1944, p. 89.

[9] 'Le Balcon', *ibid.*, p.49.

Eluard's musical voice is more modest but still haunting and harmo-
nious, and in the earlier poems at least, it announces itself on as regular a
rhythm. Alexandrines and octosyllables abound as the trigger for the
whole poem, even if the subsequent lines vary in length and rhythm. And
here in this poem, the first line is, as befits an expression of synthesis, a
perfectly balanced alexandrine with the caesura in the middle, and the
two halves reflecting symmetrically the relationship between "toi" and
"moi", a relationship which is symbolized by that initial key-word: "la
courbe" with its evocation of the feminine body combined with the
arabesque of the artist, and of that circularity which is completed when it
joins around the masculine heart. Key-word phonically also, for the
vowel sound, which echoes again in the "tour" that sets the curve into
motion, is, as one will see, to be sounded again and again throughout the
poem and to be resolved in the central "coule" of the last line.

But as well as the multiple associations implicit in this image of the
decorative and the mobile nature of feminine and artistic beauty, of the
womb-like protectiveness of the loving gaze, of the dynamic circularity
which fuses the "toi" and the "moi", I should also want to stress the
complex balance and symmetry of the structure of this motif. The second
half in fact exactly reflects the first, by its equal number of monosyllab-
les, by the way in which the stresses on "tour" and "coeur" echo those
which have occurred on "courbe" and "yeux", and by the fact that it is
the grammatical complement of the first. But, cutting across this obvious
pattern, there are other reflections and echoes which set the two halves
within the embrace of a phonic chiasmus, where the initial consonant of
courbe is echoed at the end in *cœur*, and where the vowel "eu" of "tes
yeux" in the middle of the line echoes again in more open form at the end
in "cœur". There is thus not only a statement of synthesis, but a veritable
enactment of it in image, syntax, rhythm and sound.

It is not surprisingly the key-word of the initial motif: "la courbe"
which then goes on to generate the images and sounds in lines 2 and 3
and, at the same time to attract to itself and to incorporate some facets of
basic themes dear to Eluard. The erotic, decorative, circular shape which
has been set into motion in "un rond" with its implications of fusion in
joined hands and shared rhythm; and is then given both artistic and
moral shape in the "danse de douceur", the combination of art and
moral value being further stressed by the repetition of the 'd' consonant.
That moral quality "douceur", which for Eluard was one of the most
precious adjuncts of woman, reflecting in fact the masculine heart, acts
then as the tenor of a new figure, transforming the circular shape into the

saintly luminous halo ("auréole du temps"), and at the same time adding another facet to the theme of love. Throughout Eluard's poetry, and one can see this acutely in its late manifestation in "Le Phénix", a shared love bestows a particular benediction in its sense of being "out of time". (Indeed it is a theme dear to many poets and given especial beauty by John Donne in "The Ecstasy"). Eluard's treatment, however, is characteristic, unique; and this stresses, I think, my distinction between basic theme and individual motif with its "singular" variations. For the initial vowel sound of "courbe" now develops a counterpoint in "auréole" which leads into a further transformation of the curved shape image, the "berceau" which, as the sign of the outcome of the physical fusion of line 1 consecrates it by a birth which renders safe and secure even that darkness of night which is akin to death. And here, in this opposition of the light of the halo and the dark of "nocturne", and in the recuperation of the powers of darkness by the symbol of regeneration, one can see that characteristic, basic movement of Eluard's imagination which constantly strives to pass through thesis ans antithesis in order to conquer a new synthesis. This movement is further "realised", made concrete, by the seemingly organic growth of one image out of the shape and sound of another, with the closed vowel sounds of "nocturne" and "sûr" playing their part in signifying the temporary closure of night, a closure which however is blessed by the "s" sound which has previously been linked with the "danse de douceur".

The fundamental opposition between birth and death is now developed quite differently in a logical statement, which out of two negatives set in the past, makes a positive future, and takes the basic theme of the dependence of the "moi" on the "toi" one step further. All that is contained in "savoir", memory, knowledge, wisdom, is in fact dependent on love.

This whole first verse has, as we have seen, grown out of the first word, "la courbe". The second verse is now a variation on the actual "tenor" of that initial image, "tes yeux", still maintaining the decasyllabic rhythm, and using for its series of "vehicles" elements from the natural world. Again this serves to make real another familiar strand of the love theme, namely the links between the human and the natural, and the way in which the enjoyment of a shared love gives access to a full sensual enjoyment and indeed possession of the world around. Thus, the physical qualities of the eyes give rise first to an image of fluttering luminosity: "feuilles de jour", then to the humid freshness of "mousse de rosée". It is interesting to note now that the keynote of the motif is sounding again loud and clear ("j*our*" and "m*ou*sse"). And then comes the same counterpoint that we have noted in "*auréole*", here inverted in r*oseaux*, before it returns again to the keynote in "s*ou*rires".

The imbrication of sound patterns and the associations in each successive image is here most beautifully crafted. Phonically "rosée" engenders "roseaux", and these reeds, both through metonymy (they grow next to water) and their very sound (for they could also be "roses d'eau"), trace their own variation on the theme of the fusion of human and natural, through this archetypal symbol of water back to the crucial, generating element of the "motif": "tes yeux". For the fluttering movement of the eyelids is now added to the concept of a fruitful liquidity by these reeds which are seen as tossing in the wind. The macrocosm of nature is, however, in Eluard's ideal world, always dominated by the microcosmic human being. The physical finds its culmination in the sign of a moral quality — a joyous communication — and invests it with that most evanescent halo of beauty: "sourires parfumés."

Indeed, to follow on the implications of that word "halo", it is interesting to note that the next line, the third of this verse, begins in similar fashion to line 3 of verse 1. Semantically the halo which betokens saintliness is echoed by wings, the wings of birds but also of angels; and they, like the halo are luminous and share the same function of transformation, there of time, here of space "couvrant le monde de lumière." Phonically too that 'l' of "lumière" informs both "auréole" and, even more markedly, "ailes".

It is in fact the transforming power of love which is being stressed and it is hardly surprising that the key vowel of the motif rings out in the diapason of "couvrant", which also conveys the womb-like protectiveness of that initial embrace ("le tour de mon cœur"). As if inevitably one is being led along a similar sequence to that of verse 1 in the chains of this pattern: for sure enough the next transformation of the eye image while stressing again the element of water both through metonymy and sound "bateau", reintroduces the consonant 'b' of "berceau", that image of birth which in verse 1 has appeared to be the outcome of the halo of love. Interestingly now, these "bateaux" continue the basic theme of the biopolarity of nature. For as an archetypal they tend to signify death[10], and here too they contrast directly with the airiness and mobility of the leaves and the reeds because they are bowed down under the whole

[10] cf. *Dictionnaire des Symboles*, Tome I. Seghers, 1973, p. 177.

weight of nature ("chargés du ciel et de la mer"). But, faithful to the recuperative movement so characteristic of Eluard, they go through a process of transformation, hinged on to that word "chargés". The "ch" sound, announcing connotations of passivity and stasis is turned into the "ch" of "chasseurs", the sign of activity and domination. The implied death veers first into a silence which could be that beyond the tomb or that of the ecstasy of love, transcending time and space ("chasseurs des bruits"). And then, following the organic, physical processes of "le réel" so dear to Eluard, that ecstatic moment leads inevitably to birth, birth on a cosmic scale of light itself, thus like God's creation, for it is only light which reveals colours to our senses: "Sources des couleurs". And is it any wonder that as the strands of the theme of love are being knitted together — its life-giving powers, the sharpening of perception through the eyes, the sensual enjoyment of the whole world — we are returned to the sound pattern of the motif with the repeated "ou" vowel and the "c", which by the fact that "couleurs" echoes "la courbe" joins, yet again, female beauty and art? First the arabesque now the fullness of colour. But more than that, this crucial word "couleurs", at the heart of the poem, not only reintroduces the "moi" of the poet-artist with its echo of "mon cœur", but also by its combination of sounds fuses that "cœur" with the feminine "courbe" through the middle link of the "l" of "lumière", and liquidity. I would like to suggest that this is a marvellous example both of what Riffaterre calls the obliquity of poetry, and of the sheer generative power of poetic language. The motif is unfurling, spinning out from itself its variations in order to attract the many thematic strands, and to weave them together in its decorative, recurrent patterning.

The last verse at first seems to continue the pattern of verse 2, developing the birth theme on a cosmic scale in conjunction with those "parfums", which had been previously associated with the human "sourires". But amusingly, the angelic birds too are involved in this Phœnix-like theme and honoured with the keynote of the motif ("couvée"), and the counterpoint that had invested them with sanctity of "auréole", — "aurores". The chain of opposition has however also to be worked through on the cosmic scale. I would suggest that Eluard does this by means of a word play which underlines the creative possibilities within the signifier, the ways in which ambiguities and clichés can be exploited, in order to generate meaning. It is also a way of returning to

[11] Roland Penrose: *Picasso his life and work*, Granada, 1981, p. 300.

the "oi", the poet who fills his role in the whole process of birth not merely by love but by the creation of poetry. The idea of death thus is dismissed jokily in the echo of Ci-gît, and the misery implied in the cliché "coucher sur la paille", and the word "désastres", is recuperated by this straw which is also the straw of the manger in which the Christ-child or the stars are born. Triumphantly then the night sky changes to day, which in its turn, ("jour" not surprisingly echoing "courbe"), folds back on itself to the human moral quality, "l'innocence", and thence through a tightly-knit pattern of nasals which stress the global and essential unity of "dépend", back again to "tes yeux" now endowed with the pristine purity of a world freshly born.

The relationship between "toi" and "moi" has opened up to include that between "toi" and the world in verse 2, and between "moi" and the world in verse 3. Now in this movement of diastole and of systole, the expansive flow contracts back to "mon sang", stressing its dependence with its repeated nasal sound, and linking this crucial element made mobile by the heart with the active power emanating from the eyes, "Et tout mon sang coule dans leurs regards." Notably the two poles of the initial motif have been inverted. It is now the "moi" who is the subject of the action. Thus the poem is enclosed by this overall and significant chiasmus, whose two poles are held in place by that word signifying dynamism and liquidity "coule". This then is the last variation on the keynote of the motif, which has now been endowed with life itself.

I shall now turn to a slightly different aspect of the use of the motif and its variations, and here, I think, my chosen examples are paradoxical and particularly challenging. So far, I may have seemed to be giving prime emphasis to the sound patterns instituted by the motif. But with the two short poems which begin identically with "L'oreille du taureau à la fenêtre", it is abundantly clear that the origins also lie in the pictorial. Even if one were not familiar with the various avatars of the bull in the paintings of Picasso, throughout his career but particlarly from the late 30's onwards, the fact that the first poem occurs as Section IV of the suite entitled *A Pablo Picasso* published in *Donner à Voir* in 1939, would associate it firmly with the iconography of this particular painter.

Now this inevitably brings up the whole question of the relationship between the visual arts and poetry, and this is of course a vast subject. All I can do here is to high-light certain points. First, in Picasso's work the bull is a most enigmatic figure. Critics have interpreted it in many different ways. Is he a victim or monster, is he the painter himself? Is he the Spanish people? In Guernica he seems to be standing impassively detached. Does he then signify the unintended cruelty of neutrality? The most generally accepted interpretation is perforce the most general one — that he seems to represent destiny itself." This then would account for his different guises.

However Eluard dismembers the Picasso bull and concentrates on only one part of him — the bull's ear put in prominence in front of the window. Now although critics, and in particular Jean-Charles Gateau, have tried to identify various bull's ears put in a prominent position in Picasso's paintings[12], there does not seem to be any one very convincing example. I personally think the poet's point of departure is not so closely linked with an actual visual detail taken from one painting. The bull motif in general certainly belongs to Picasso, thus signifies Picasso, and the poems of *Donner à Voir* are addressed to Picasso, but this particular bull's ear in the window belongs to Eluard. Detached from its owner, it has presumably been cut off. Now the ear is traditionally cut from the dead, vanquished bull and given to the matador as a sign of his victory. Thus it is both the sign of a defeat and of a victory. It is moreover placed in the full light of the window. However, windows look both inwards and outwards. This motif, undoubtedly inspired by Picasso, has, I would suggest, a more specific symbolism than the painting, but at its first appearance it is redolent with ambiguity and paradox.

But here, in fact, the hermeneutic task is made easier because of its position in the whole sequence of poems which unequivocally celebrate Picasso's positive and original contribution, his creative triumph against those who have "inventé l'ennui" or the superficiality of "le rire". The first poem has been called by Jean-Charles Gateau[13] — and rightly I think — an anti-Baudelaire, and certainly its last line 'C'en est fini des joies greffées sur le chagrin" would seem to refer to *Les Fleurs du Mal*, just as the last line of the second section: "A ta vue je sais que rien n'est perdu" is a clear stance against all those who like Proust claim that "les vrais paradis sont les paradis qu'on a perdus". The last line of the third section, i.e. the one immediately preceding "L'oreille du taureau" is indeed the unambiguous, "La fête est nouvelle." Therefore I would propose to see in this motif taken from Picasso's painting a celebration of a victory which is in some way related to him and to his art. There is, however, another fact which strikes me about this first-line motif... As well as signalling so very clearly to the pictorial reference, like so many of

[12] Jean-Charles Gateau: *Eluard, Picasso et la Peinture*, 1936 — 52. Droz, 1983, p. 83.
[13] *ibid.*, p. 35.

Eluard's first lines it has a haunting musical quality, and this is due largely to the repetition of the "au" sound in "taureau" and its interplay with the open 'o" of "l'oreille". Not surprisingly with such a careful craftsman as Eluard, it is then with an inversion of that same interplay of sounds that the motif is developed. The "au" of "taureau" is repeated again in the centre of the second line with "sauvage", a word also linked with it semantically, and the open "o" of the initial "oreille" echoes again in that structure of phonic chiasmus which Eluard so often favours, in "soleil blessé". Thus the taureau is linked with the primitive, and the sign of defeat with the wounded sun. It would seem that it is almost with the purpose of identifying it that the sun is now specified as un soleil d'intérieur and that that particular word is linked back to the "taureau" by its consonants, which resonate again in the stressed last word "se terre." The combination of bull, earth symbol if there ever was one, savagery, the primitive, some kind of interior illumination under the sign of defeat, is being worked out at all levels.

The final couplet however takes up the crucial consonants of the defeated "taureau" and the "eil" of l'oreille, but develops them in that dialectical movement which we have already noted in Eluard, to celebrate the other pole, that of victory, "Tentures du réveil". It is an awakening which has to do with the decorative, and in which the actual reality of the bedroom, transformed most royally as "parois", has conquered the interior world of sleep. And again it is no coincidence that the word "sommeil" (notably not the more positive, creative part of it, "le rêve") echoes closely, semantically and phonically, the "soleil blessé", the "soleil d'intérieur". It seems to me clear that the senses of primitivity, an interior scene, a sickly illumination, sleep, are pointing towards an identification of the bull figure of the motif with the enclosure in the interior primitive world of the unconscious that characterized Surrealism. Despite its own kind of illumination ("un soleil d'intérieur") Eluard is now celebrating the way in which his friend has on the contrary helped to open up the possibilities of a positive communion with the material world ("on est ami avec l'homme et la bête" he had said in Section IV). If the first section is an anti-Baudelaire, I would suggest that this fourth section takes the evolutionary process further and celebrates Eluard's own emergence from the solipsistic inner world of Surrealism.

Victory/defeat: it is impossible I think to separate the motif of the bull's ear at the window from this overall theme. But whose victory and whose defeat, and which side are you on? I would suggest that it is precisely because of these ambiguities that Eluard chose this same line to trigger off another and quite different poem published in *Poésie and Vérité* in 1942. It is again linked inevitably with Picasso, but at a very different juncture, when Picasso during the Occupation was in fact using the bull image obsessively and sometimes even as a sort of Beast of the Apocalypse to symbolize the oppressor. The fact of his using it however, exemplifies the defiant nature of his creativity, the possibility it holds of the victory of the spirit. Defeat then turned into victory, but not yet overt: and the ambiguities in this double-bind make, of course, a perfect cover for the "contrebande" so familiar to the war poets.

So the poem announces itself with the resonance of its open vowels, and the added connotations of victory which had accrued to it from its use in the joyful Picasso celebratory poem. But instead of developing the first element of the image it is now the second element "la fenêtre" which is used as the hinge for the next variation, and this variation is based on a definite pattern of bipolarity. The bull's ear, the present-day light and the straw of the vanquished are all ranged at the beginning of each line under the symbol of defeat, but the right-hand side of each line transforms each of those negative elements into their positive manifestation. The possibility of illumination present in the window element of the motif, becomes the ambiguous "prisme de la force", the prism which like the window allows light through, but deforms it, deflects it, as it can deflect the strength of the present-day, the strength of an oppressor. The process of deflection turns then into a triumphant metamorphosis, the "p" sound of prisme leading into "la paille du vaincu". This straw of poverty is, as we have already noticed, also a sign of birth, and the deflected light now transforms this straw into gold. Again the sound pattern is weaving its own oblique meaning. The defeat implicit in the "*o*reille du t*au*reau" has been transformed into the victory of those same sounds in "*l'o*r du p*au*vre."

As in the previous poem the scene now shifts to this side of the window, the interior of the house, the house presumably of the "pauvre". Again there would seem to be a reference to the still-life paintings of Picasso with "table" "vin" and "bouteille". Jean-Charles Gateau goes so far as to try to identify these still-lifes, seeing for instance a loving portrait of Dora Maar as a proof of the painter's eye "qui saisit la bouche et l'embrasse"[14]. I would personally like to stress the way in which the partially filled bottle of wine — an ironic symbol of the deprivations of wartime, yet still a comfort, — is linked to the "l'or*e*ille

[14] *ibid.*, p. 83.

du t*au*re*au*" by the echoing sounds of "nive*au*" and "bout*eille*"; and also the way in which that table and the wine could well evoke also, at a different "niveau", the Last Supper. It would indeed be an entirely appropriate expression of Eluard's fundamental theme of humanism, to defy man and beast by seeing the blood from the wounded ear as being transformed into wine. This divine power of transformation is also the primordial quality which he often praises in Picasso, the supreme example of the artist-creator, and which he chooses to celebrate with religious imagery ("Sous ton teint renversé la coupole et la hache de ton front" in *Donner à Voir*). And indeed it is the loving and active eye which effects the next sudden miraculous metamorphosis which must be received also by the organ of sight. "Et regarde il fait beau." The light of "aujourd'hui" has been made beautiful, and the taureau is in the process of becoming that "beau taureau" who is about to appear so meaningfully in line 8.

But first comes an important, indeed crucial, development of the theme of the transforming power of an art which is informed by love. For the seeds which have been sown by that look of Picasso are now to ferment in the "sillon du laboureur sanglant." And here I think that Gateau is absolutely right[15] to detect an echo of the Marseillaise and thus, in this alexandrine at the heart of the poem, to discern a call to arms. The blood here is not the impure blood of the enemy, but that of the unidentified ploughman followed by "le taureau le beau taureau" so unfortunately "lourd de désastres", who will however plough the furrow of future victory. It is a most beautiful and poignant line, and to my mind indicates exactly which side Eluard is on. This magnificent but unfortunate beast is, in fact, the people of France. That word "beau" is applied first to the sunlight then to the "taureau", then again to the outside world. The interior humble scene of defeat and deprivation has opened out on to the outside world, a world informed by the crucial quality of love. And that vowel sound which had previously been associated with the negative heaviness of misfortune: "l*ou*rd de désas-tres", is now reiterated three times in "la b*ou*che *ou*verte à l'am*ou*r". Having then been endowed with the associations of generosity and love, and according to the characteristic dialectical workings of Eluard's poetry, it re-emerges in a new third term, the synthesis of the natural world. The heaviness of the bull's misfortune has now been turned into the heaviness of the cloud which actually supports the sun in the

[15] *ibid.*, p. 82.

inevitable cycle of nature. The French people are being encouraged by the patterns of the natural world to follow those leaders who have died or are dying for it ("le sang du laboureur"), and out of the seeds of misfortune to make "le pain des noces'." This evocation of the staff of life, of the loving and giving of this future wedding feast, completes the variation on the theme of the Last Supper introduced in verse 2. The death announced in that ultimate feast has turned into the joy of the wedding of Cana, where Christ *first* worked a miracle. The parsimonious level of the wine in the bottle has been transformed into brimming casks and that last word "n*oces*" resonates once more with the initial sign of defeat "*oreille*", changing it into joy and a victorious and fruitful communion.

This, however, is a future vision. The last verse of the poem returns once more to the "taureau" and the sounds associated with him in a new image of present-day struggle "le drapeau du taureau". This simple evocation of the emblematic flag stretched taut in the wind like a sword is indeed a rallying cry. The open sounds associated with the motif of the bull's ear have been transformed by tension into the closed sounds and the pointed shape of the "épée". And yet again, at the close of the poem as at its inception, there is the presence of Pablo Picasso. For Eluard, the agressive nature of the painter, the necessary destruction he wreaks before creating the new, have always been associated with the imagery of battle. (To quote only one example taken again from *Donner à Voir*: "Derrière ton regard avec trois épées croisées / Tes cheveux nattent le vent rebelle").

The bizarre and ambiguous bull's ear motif, then, has nucleated to include the historical instance — the misfortunes of the French people and the call to arms — but also the moral themes so dear to Eluard, of love and generosity, of the oneness of man and the natural world, and of an optimism which is based on an essential faith in the creative spirit of man, here evidenced in poetry as well as in the painting of his friend.

I began by quoting from *Avenir de la Poésie*. I can find no better way to conclude than by coming back to Eluard's own words in that text: "Le pain est plus utile que la poésie. Mais l'amour au sens complet, humain du mot, l'amour-passion n'est pas plus utile que la poésie." And again: "Pas un jeu de mots. Tout est comparable à tout, tout trouve son écho, sa raison, sa ressemblance, son opposition, son devenir partout. Et ce devenir est infini." [16]

---

[16] cf. *Œuvres complètes*, Tome I, p. 527.

Constantin FLOROS

(Universität Hamburg)

ÜBER DEN MOTIVBEGRIFF IN DER MUSIKWISSENSCHAFT

I

VORBEMERKUNGEN

Seit ihrer Grundlegung durch Alexander Baumgarten ist es ein Anliegen der Ästhetik, sowohl die Gemeinsamkeiten als auch die Unterschiede zwischen den schönen Künsten zu erforschen. Überblickt man eine Reihe repräsentativer Meinungen, so wird man finden, daß das Interesse der meisten Denker darauf gerichtet ist, das Spezifische jeder Kunst zu ergründen, anders formuliert, die Grenzen zwischen den einzelnen Künsten abzustecken. Freilich hat es auch nicht an Versuchen gefehlt, das einigende Band zwischen den Künsten sichtbar zu machen, die Affinitäten zwischen ihnen zu beleuchten. Zu den Grundgedanken romantischer Kunsttheorie, wie sie die Brüder Schlegel, Jean Paul und E. Th. A. Hoffmann entwickelten, gehören die Auffassungen, daß die Poesie Inbegriff jeder Kunst sei und daß Musik und Poesie, die „romantischsten" Künste, eng miteinander verwandt seien. Robert Schumann, den man zu den Romantikern wird zählen dürfen, prägte den Satz „Die Ästhetik der einen Kunst ist die der andern"[1] und erregte damit den Unmut Eduard Hanslicks[2].

Die Thematologie ist ein Gegenstand, an dem man das Verhältnis zwischen den Künsten besonders gut studieren kann. Zählen doch die Termini Motiv, Thema, Sujet und Stoff zu den Begriffen, die in fast allen Künsten eine wichtige Rolle spielen. Als besonders eng und aufschlußreich erweisen sich in dieser Hinsicht die Beziehungen zwischen der Musik und der Literatur, weil es zwischen ihnen zur gegenseitigen Befruchtung und zu einem Austauschprozeß kam. Die Leitmotivtechnik Richard Wagners erregte die Aufmerksamkeit vieler Schriftsteller und wurde auch in der Literatur heimisch. Umgekehrt drangen zumal im 19.

---

[1] Robert Schumann: Gesammelte Schriften über Musik und Musiker, 5. Aufl. hrsg. von Martin Kreisig, Band I, Leipzig 1914, S. 26.

[2] Eduard Hanslick: Vom Musikalisch-Schönen. Ein Beitrag zur Revision der Ästhetik der Tonkunst, 12. Aufl. Leipzig 1918, S. 3.

Jahrhundert literarische Ideen in die Musik ein. Sie beeinflußten die
Konzeptionen führender Komponisten und trugen wesentlich zur Ver-
breitung des Musikdramas und der Programmusik bei. Man muß diesen
Sachverhalt stets in Betracht ziehen, wenn man Erörterungen über den
Motivbegriff in der Musik anstellt.

Der Terminus Motiv wird im musikanalytischen und im musikwissen-
schaftlichen Schrifttum so oft verwendet, daß es wirklich verwunderlich
wäre, wenn er in einer einheitlichen Auffassung begegnen würde. Sichtet
man eine größere Anzahl an Definitionen, so kristallisieren sich drei
Bedeutungsvarianten heraus, nämlich:

Motiv erstens als die Hauptidee einer Komposition — eine Auffassung, die Jean-Jacques Rousseau vertrat;

Motiv zweitens als Bauelement einer Komposition, d.h. als kleinstes
Einheitsglied ohne bestimmte Semantik und

Motiv drittens im Sinne von Leitmotiv und von charakteristischem
Motiv, d.h. als eine musikalische Gestalt, der eine bestimmte außermusikalische Semantik beigegeben ist.

Fassen wir diese drei Bedeutungsvarianten des Begriffs näher ins
Auge.

II

DAS MOTIV ALS HAUPTIDEE UND ALS BAUELEMENT EINER KOMPOSITION

Wesentliche Informationen über die Motivauffassung im 18. Jahrhundert verdanken wir dem „Dictionnaire de musique" von Jean-Jacques
Rousseau, einem Buch, das in erster Auflage 1767 und in zweiter Auflage
1781 erschien. In dem einschlägigen Artikel[3] berichtet Rousseau, daß der
Terminus Motiv italienischer Herkunft sei und daß er zu seiner Zeit fast
ausschließlich im technischen Sinne von Komponisten gebraucht werde
Einige Dezennien später scheint sich die Situation geändert zu haben,
denn Goethe verwendet schon in den neunziger Jahren das Wort in einer
Bedeutung, an die später die Literaturwissenschaft anknüpfen konnte.
Unter einem Motiv versteht Rousseau in erster Linie die ursprüngliche
und Hauptidee, durch die ein Komponist sein Sujet bestimmt und seinen
Plan festlegt. Dabei hat er das Moment des Antriebs und des Bewegungs-
anstoßes im Sinn, denn er sagt ausdrücklich, das Motiv gebe dem
Komponisten die Feder in die Hand, damit er diese Sache und nicht eine

---

[3] Jean-Jacques Rousseau: Dictionnaire de musique, 2. Aufl. Genf 1781, Band I, S. 500f.

andere zu Papier bringe. In diesem Sinne müsse das Motiv im Geiste des Komponisten stets gegenwärtig sein, und er müsse es derart behandeln, daß es auch im Geiste der Zuhörer gegenwärtig bleibe. Neben dieser Begriffsauffassung gebe es auch besondere Motive, die die Modulation, die Verflechtungen und die harmonische Textur bestimmten.

Im 19. Jahrhundert wurde der Terminus Motiv zu einem Grundbegriff deutscher Kompositionslehren[4], verlor jedoch dabei die allgemeine Bedeutung, die er bei Rousseau hatte. Zwar sprechen auch deutsche Theoretiker im Zusammenhang mit einem Motiv vielfach vom Keim, Trieb und Bewegungsanstoß einer Komposition[5], sie beziehen jedoch den Terminus auf die Melodie und verstehen darunter nicht mehr die Hauptidee einer Komposition, sondern ein wichtiges Bauelement, genauer gesagt: den Bestandteil eines musikalischen Themas. Das Motiv wird als „Keim thematischen Gestaltens"[6], als „kleinstes Glied"[7] und als „kleine Einheit"[8] einer Komposition definiert. Diese Bedeutung des Terminus ist die konventionellste und am weitesten verbreitete. Sie begegnet in fast allen musikalischen Formenlehren bis heute. Viele Autoren suchen den Umfang der Motive näher zu bestimmen, das Verhältnis von Motiv und Thema zu umreißen und die Behandlungsmöglichkeiten der Motive zu exemplifizieren[9]. Besondere Bedeutung in diesem Zusammenhang kommt der sogenannten motivisch-thematischen Arbeit zu, einer Technik, die zuerst in den Werken Haydns, Mozarts und vor allem Beethovens einen hohen Standard erreichte. Gemeint ist das Verfahren, die Motive eines Satzes in den Durchführungspartien aufzugreifen, zu verarbeiten, zu variieren, abzuspalten, zu entwickeln, in neuen Beleuchtungen erscheinen zu lassen, gegenüberzustellen und miteinander kontrapunktisch zu verflechten. Der ausgesprochen dynamische Charakter der Durchführungsteile in der Musik des 18. bis 20. Jahrhunderts resultiert folgerichtig aus der Energetik, die musikalischen Motiven innewohnt.

[4] Siehe etwa J.C. Lobe: Lehrbuch der musikalischen Komposition, 2. Aufl., Erster Band, Leipzig 1858, S. 11. Vgl. dazu Hugo Riemann: Was ist ein Motiv?, in: Präludien und Studien, Band I, Leipzig o. J. [1895], S. 137-149.

[5] Adolf Bernhard Marx: Die Lehre von der musikalischen Komposition. Neu bearbeitet von Hugo Riemann, Band I, 9. Aufl. Leipzig 1887, S. 32.

[6] Hans Heinrich Eggebrecht (Hrsg.): Riemann Musiklexikon. Sachteil, Artikel Thema, Mainz 1967, S. 950.

[7] Ebenda, Artikel Motiv, S. 591.

[8] Hans Pfitzner: Die neue Ästhetik der musikalischen Impotenz, München 1920, S. 58f.

[9] Vgl. dazu Hugo Leichtentritt: Musikalische Formenlehre, 2. Aufl. Leipzig 1920, S. 235-237.

Die energetische Funktion musikalischer Motive legt einen Vergleich mit der Eigenart literarischer Motive nahe, die mitunter gleichfalls als stoffliche bzw. strukturelle Einheiten angesprochen werden[10]. Führt man einen solchen Vergleich durch, so treten sogleich mindestens zwei gravierende Unterschiede zutage. Im Gegensatz zur literaturwissenschaftlichen Verwendung des Terminus werden in der traditionellen musikalischen Formenlehre nahezu alle Bausteine einer Komposition Motive genannt, ungeachtet der Frage, wie profiliert und charakteristisch sie sind. Bedenkt man nun, daß den großen Werken der klassisch-romantischen Musik, etwa den Symphonien und Sonaten, eine Fülle kontrastierender Themen und Motive zugrunde liegt, so hat diese Gepflogenheit eine relative Unschärfe des Begriffs zur Folge. Nur selten bauen neuere Komponisten umfangreiche Sätze auf wenigen Motiven oder gar auf einem einzigen Motiv auf, wie dies Beethoven im Kopfsatz seiner Fünften Symphonie getan hat. Ein zweiter Unterschied: In der sogenannten absoluten Musik und auch in solcher Musik, die für absolut gehalten wird, haben die Motive keine Semantik im Sinne der Wortsemantik, wenngleich ihnen stets ein Ausdrucksgehalt innewohnt. So verglich denn auch Hugo Riemann[11] die musikalischen Motive mit „mimischen Gesten" und definierte: „Ein Motiv ist also ein Melodiebruchstück, das für sich eine kleinste Einheit von selbständiger Ausdrucksbedeutung bildet, die einzelne Geste des musikalischen Ausdrucks."

III

ZUR SPRACHÄHNLICHKEIT DER MUSIK

Die Feststellung, daß eine Klasse von Motiven einer ausgeprägten Semantik im Sinne der Wortsemantik entbehrt, führt uns zur wichtigen Frage nach dem Verhältnis von Musik und Sprache. Die Meinungen darüber gehen weit auseinander. Während viele Forscher die Musik als eine Art Sprache auffassen und von ihrer Sprachähnlichkeit und ihrem

---

[10] Gero von Wilpert: Sachwörterbuch der Literatur, 5. Aufl. Stuttgart 1969, S. 498; Elisabeth Frenzel: Stoff-, Motiv- und Symbolforschung, 4. Aufl. Stuttgart 1978, S. 29. Vgl auch Willy Krogmann, Artikel Motiv, in: Reallexikon der deutschen Literaturgeschichte, hrsg. von Werner Kohlschmidt und Wolfgang Mohr, Zweiter Band, Berlin 1965, S. 427-432.

[11] Hugo Riemann: System der musikalischen Rhythmik und Metrik, Leipzig 1903, S. 14.

sprachhaften Charakter reden[12], halten andere jeden Vergleich mit der Sprache für verfehlt[13]. Der Dissens resultiert sowohl aus der Komplexität des Problems selbst als auch aus den divergierenden ästhetischen Positionen, die die einzelnen Autoren einnehmen.

Redet man von der Sprachähnlichkeit der Musik, so sollte man nicht vergessen zu präzisieren, welche Art Musik man meint. In dieser Hinsicht bestehen nämlich überaus signifikante Unterschiede. So wird die einstimmige liturgische Musik des Mittelalters, der gregorianische Choral, zu Recht als eine Art von Textaussprache definiert. Als solche unterscheidet sich diese Musik grundsätzlich etwa von der konzertanten Musik des Barock, die man wohl als Spiel auffassen kann. Auf sie paßt einigermaßen Eduard Hanslicks Aperçu vom Inhalt der Musik als von „tönend bewegter Formen". Die konzertante Musik des 18. und 19. Jahrhunderts ist aber ganz anders beschaffen als die Ausdrucksmusik eines Wagner, Bruckner und Mahler. Ihr wird man sprachhaften Charakter wohl attestieren müssen.

Im 18. und zumal im 19. Jahrhundert galt die Musik vielfach als Sprache des Gefühls, des Herzens, der Seele. Für Robert Schumann war poetische Musik — wie für Hegel — „Seelensprache"[14]. Um die Musik von der Dichtung abzugrenzen, griffen viele zu der Formel, wonach der Ton das Gefühl affiziere, wogegen das Wort sich primär an den Verstand wende. Die Formel enthält einen richtigen Kern, und doch trifft sie nicht ganz zu. Zwar ist die starke emotive Wirkung der Musik, ihre Fähigkeit, Gefühle zu erregen, seit dem Altertum bekannt und unbestreitbar. Daneben darf man jedoch nicht übersehen, daß sie als Struktur sich an den Verstand wendet und auch die Vorstellung anspricht.

Die Musik besitzt — wie bereits Franz Liszt treffend bemerkte — ihre eigene Grammatik, Logik, Syntax und Rhetorik sowie ein Vokabular, das ständiger Wandlung unterworfen ist. Das ist der Bereich, der Vergleiche mit der Sprache ermöglicht. Bezeichnenderweise orientierte sich die Theorie der mittelalterlichen Musik zu einem wesentlichen Teil an der Grammatik. Die Terminologie der neueren musikalischen For-

---

[12] Theodor W. Adorno: Fragment über Musik und Sprache, in: Quasi una fantasia. Musikalische Schriften II, Frankfurt am Main 1963, S. 9-16; Klaus Wolfgang Niemöller: Der sprachhafte Charakter der Musik (Rheinisch-Westfälische Akademie der Wissenschaften. Geisteswissenschaften. Vorträge. G 244), Opladen 1980, S. 52-56.

[13] Roland Harweg: Noch einmal: Sprache und Musik, in: Poetica, 1967, Nr. 1, S. 556-566.

[14] Dazu Constantin Floros: Schumanns musikalische Poetik, in: Musik-Konzepte. Sonderband Robert Schumann I, München 1981, S. 90-104.

menlehre ist weitgehend der Syntax entlehnt; so sprechen wir von Sätzen und Halbsätzen, von Phrasen und Perioden. Und gleichfalls sprechen wir von musikalischer Logik. Darunter verstehen wir die Kunst, musikalische Gedanken folgerichtig zu entwickeln. Johannes Brahms zum Beispiel wurde und wird als Meister strenger musikalischer Logik gerühmt.

Ein wichtiger Punkt, an dem sich die Musik von der Sprache unterscheidet, ist die Semantik. Im Gegensatz zur Sprache, die über eine geschärfte Semantik verfügt, ist die Musik von Hause aus semantisch vage. Gleichwohl haben viele Komponisten zu allen Zeiten es verstanden, ihre Musik zu semantisieren. Das gelang ihnen durch Zitate, durch Anspielungen auf eigene und auf fremde Werke, durch musikalisch-rhetorische Figuren und vor allem durch Leitmotive und „charakteristische" Motive. Da diese beiden Gruppen von Motiven für die interdisziplinäre Forschung besondere Relevanz besitzen, werden sie im Mittelpunkt der folgenden Ausführungen stehen.

IV

ZUR FUNKTION DES LEITMOTIVS BEI RICHARD WAGNER

Die Leitmotivtechnik Richard Wagners ist ein Verfahren gewesen, welches das Musikdrama des ausgehenden 19. und 20. Jahrhunderts entscheidend beeinflußte und überdies in die Literatur Eingang fand[15]. Gleichwohl herrschen über sein Wesen immer noch verheerende Mißverständnisse. Die spöttischen Bemerkungen Claude Debussys und Igor Strawinskys zeugen von tiefer Verständnislosigkeit. Es will scheinen, als hätte erst Thomas Mann die wahren Intentionen Wagners erkannt. In seinen Essays finden wir jedenfalls die tiefsten Einsichten in das Wesen des Leitmotivs. Thomas Mann, der bekannte, von Wagner unheimlich viel gelernt zu haben, bewunderte in ihm nicht nur den „leidenschaftlichen Theatraliker", Mythiker und Psychologen, sondern auch einen großen Epiker. Der „Ring des Nibelungen" ist nach Mann ein „szenisches Epos", ein Werk, das seine Großartigkeit dem „epischen Kunstgeist" verdankt und zugleich ein Werk, in dem Wagners „thematisch-motivische Gewebstechnik" Triumphe feiert. Sinn dieser Technik sei es geistvoll-tiefsinnige Beziehungen herzustellen und das „Themen-

---

[15] Der vorliegende Abschnitt über Richard Wagner stützt sich auf meinen Aufsatz: Der „Beziehungszauber" der Musik im „Ring des Nibelungen" von Richard Wagner, in: Neue Zeitschrift für Musik, 144. Jg., Juli/August 1983, S. 8-14.

Gewebe" nicht nur über eine Szene und über ein Drama, sondern über die ganze Tetralogie sich ausbreiten zu lassen.

Wagner selbst hatte schon 1851 in seinem Aufsatz „Eine Mitteilung an meine Freunde" die Grundzüge seines Verfahrens erläutert[16]. Seine Ausführungen fanden indes nicht immer die nötige Beachtung. In diesem Aufsatz schildert er, wie er von den traditionellen Opernformen wegkam und zu Formungen gelangte, die der Natur seiner Stoffe und der für sie erforderlichen Darstellungsweise angemessen waren. Dabei gibt er deutlich zu verstehen, daß seine Leitmotivtechnik (er gebraucht diesen Terminus selbst nicht) primär ein literarisches Verfahren war. Während der Arbeit am „Tannhäuser" und noch entschiedener am „Lohengrin" sei er zur Einsicht gekommen, daß in einer der entscheidenden Szenen des Dramas keine „Stimmung" angeschlagen werden durfte, „die nicht in einem wichtigen Bezuge zu den Stimmungen der anderen Szenen stand". Dementsprechend galt es ein „Gewebe" von musikalischen Hauptthemen zu bilden, das sich „in innigster Beziehung zur dichterischen Absicht" über das ganze Drama ausbreitete.

Der „Ring des Nibelungen" nun ist das erste Werk Wagners, in dem die Leitmotivtechnik konsequent durchgeführt ist. Wagner legte der Tetralogie eine größere Anzahl von Leitmotiven zugrunde, die exponiert, fortgesponnen, verändert, neu gruppiert, neu beleuchtet, miteinander kombiniert und symphonisch verarbeitet werden. Dabei gibt es Motive, die in allen vier Teilen des Bühnenfestspiels wiederkehren, und andere wiederum, die nur einzelnen Dramen vorbehalten sind.

Unterzieht man die Motive einer semantischen Untersuchung, so kann man feststellen, daß sie Verschiedenartiges bezeichnen: Personen, Urelemente, Gegenstände, Empfindungen, Affekte, Leidenschaften, Naturzustände, Ideen. In Korrespondenz zu den Verwicklungen des Nibelungenmythos, den Wagner zu einer Welttragödie gestaltete, umfassen sie den ganzen Kosmos des Seienden, nahezu das Universum der deutschen Mythologie.

Bedenkt man, daß literarische Motive oft situationsmäßige Elemente und Handlungsansätze bilden, so kann man sich über die vielen Motive bei Wagner wundern, die konkrete Personen und Gegenstände bezeichnen. Man versteht indessen seine Intentionen besser, wenn man erst erkannt hat, daß selbst diesen Motiven stets Seelisches und Symbolisches anhaftet. Das Siegfriedmotiv zum Beispiel symbolisiert nicht nur die

---

[16] Richard Wagner: Sämtliche Schriften und Dichtungen, 6. Aufl. Leipzig o. J., Band IV, S. 322.

Person Siegfrieds. sondern auch die Idee des Heldentums, das Heroische. Das Ringmotiv ist ein Sinnbild für Macht und Machtstreben. Das Schwertmotiv konnotiert Schutz und Sieg usf.

Wie kaum ein anderer Komponist des neunzehnten Jahrhunderts hat Wagner die Musik psychologisiert und semantisiert. Überaus hilfreich für ein tieferes Verständnis seiner Leitmotivtechnik sind seine Ausführungen in seinem Buch „Oper und Drama', speziell im dritten Teil, wo er auf das Verhältnis von Dichtkunst und Tonkunst eingeht[17]. Angelpunkt seiner Erörterungen ist das Verhältnis von Wort- und Tonsprache, von Gedanke und Empfindung, von „Versmelodie" und Orchester. Dabei unterscheidet er drei Stationen des dramatischen Ausdrucks: die Ahnung, die Vergegenwärtigung und die Erinnerung. Von Vergegenwärtigung spricht Wagner, wenn der Darsteller einen Gedanken mitteilt und der latent in diesem enthaltenen Empfindung durch die gesungene Melodie Ausdruck verleiht. Greift das Orchester zu einem späteren Zeitpunkt des Dramas diese Melodie (das heißt: ein bestimmtes Motiv) auf, so erinnert sich der Hörer an jenen Gedanken; dadurch erhält die Musik außermusikalische Bedeutung. In anderen Fällen wiederum nimmt das Orchester eine gedanklich noch nicht ausgesprochene Stimmung vorweg. Wagner spricht dann von „Ahnung". Die Musik des „Ring" ist voller solcher Erinnerungen und Ahnungen, voller Anspielungen auf Künftiges und Dagewesenes. Das Leitmotiv erfüllt sowohl eine erinnernde als auch eine wahrsagerische Funktion.

Vergegenwärtigung und Erinnerung lassen sich wohl am besten am Beispiel des Fluchmotivs verdeutlichen. Der Fluchgedanke gehört zu jenen Motiven, die sich gleich roten Fäden durch die ganze Tetralogie ziehen. Zuerst wird er in der vierten Rheingold-Szene ausgesprochen. Wotan und Loge haben Alberich mit List gefangengenommen. Um seine Freiheit zu erlangen, muß Alberich alles hergeben, was er hat: den Hort, die Tarnkappe und auch den Ring. Seine erste Tat, als Loge ihm die Bande löst, ist, den Ring zu verfluchen: „Wie durch Fluch er mir geriet, verflucht sei dieser Ring", ruft er bei Paukentremolo zu den Tönen des Fluchmotivs aus.

Nur ein wenig später werden wir mit einer ähnlichen Situation konfrontiert: Um Freia zu befreien, müssen jetzt die Götter den Riesen den Hort, die Tarnkappe und auch den Ring überlassen. Im Streit um den Ring erschlägt Fafner seinen Bruder Fasolt. Da tönt im Orchester (als erste Erinnerung an Alberichs Fluch) das Fluchmotiv, und Wotan —

[17] Ebenda, Band IV, S. 186-192.

im Tiefsten erschüttert — kommentiert: „Furchtbar nun erfind' ich des Fluches Kraft!"

Dem Fluch Alberichs entgeht keiner der Besitzer des Rings: weder Fafner noch Siegfried. Im Streit um den Ring fällt Gunther, und selbst Hagen wird zum Opfer des Fluches seines Vaters. Erst nachdem der Ring durch Brünnhildes Feuertod in den Besitz der Rheintöchter zurückgelangt, verliert der Fluch seine Macht: ein Fragment des Fluchmotivs klingt im Orchester auf, dann verstummt der Fluch für immer.

Tiefe Einblicke in das Wesen und die psychologische Funktion der Leitmotivik gewähren vor allem doppelbödige Aussagen bei Wagner. Gemeint sind Fälle, wo die Aussage des Darstellers semantisch mit jener des Orchesters nicht übereinzustimmen scheint. Zur Veranschaulichung des Sachverhalts gebrauchte Ernst Bloch[18] das Bild von einem Ablauf der Ereignisse in zwei Stockwerken: in manchen Fällen spricht und handelt der gesungene Text oben — so meinte Bloch — durchaus nicht dort, wo das Leitmotiv der Musik im unteren Stockwerk spricht und handelt.

Ein aufschlußreiches Beispiel für diesen Sachverhalt finden wir im zweiten Siegfried-Aufzug, und zwar in der zweiten Szene. Um Siegfried das Fürchten zu lehren, führt ihn Mime an die Höhle Fafners. Mimes eindringliche Schilderung der Gefährlichkeit des Drachen macht auf den jungen Helden gar keinen Eindruck. Im Orchester dominieren Fafner-motive— man muß sagen: logischerweise, denn Fafner ist der Gegenstand des Gesprächs. An zwei Stellen klingt allerdings im Orchester überraschenderweise das Motiv der schlummernden Brünnhilde auf — überraschenderweise, denn die auf dem Felsen schlafende und vom Feuermeer umgebene Walküre steht in keinem direkten Zusammenhang mit dem Thema des Gesprächs. Erst wenn man genauer auf den Sinn der Worte achtet, erkennt man, daß Wagner hier so etwas wie eine Psychoanalyse des Leitmotivs leistet: Mimes Worte beziehen sich auf die Furcht, die der Wurm einzujagen vermag. Dadurch aber, daß das Orchester diese Worte mit dem Motiv Brünnhildes untermalt, leuchtet die Musik ins Unbewußte und deckt auf, daß Siegfried sich nur vor der Liebe fürchtet. Thomas Mann hatte sicherlich Recht, als er einmal bemerkte, als Psychologe berühre sich Wagner mit Sigmund Freud, ja, er stimme mit ihm in merkwürdigster, „intuitiver" Weise überein.

---

[18] Ernst Bloch: Paradoxa und Pastorale bei Wagner, in: Zur Philosophie der Musik, Frankfurt am Main 1974, S. 246.

Fluch und Untergang gehören im „Ring" zusammen. Vom Fluch Alberichs sind auch die Götter betroffen. Weil sie unfrei, furchtsam und ohnmächtig geworden sind, müssen sie untergehen. Der Gedanke vom herbeigesehnten, ja gewollten Ende durchzieht leitmotivisch die Tetralogie. Im Rheingold exponiert, wird er in der Walküre und im Siegfried konsequent weiterentwickelt und in der Götterdämmerung zu Ende geführt. Zur plastischen Darstellung des Gedankens setzt Wagner vier Leitmotive ein: das Motiv der Nornen, die ja Schicksalsgöttinnen sind, das Motiv der Götterdämmerung, das Motiv der Zerstörung und das Ringmotiv. Sie alle tönen bereits in der vierten Rheingold-Szene auf, als Erda — die allwissende Seherin und Mutter der Nornen — auftaucht, Wotan vor dem Fluch des Rings warnt und das Ende der Götter prophezeit. Der Untergang der Götter its bereits im ersten Teil der Tetralogie vorprogrammiert.

V

„CHARAKTERISTISCHE" MOTIVE IN DER SYMPHONISCHEN MUSIK

Plastizität, psychologische Funktion und Symbolträchtigkeit sind Eigenschaften der Wagnerschen Leitmotive, jedoch nicht nur ihrer. Gleichzeitig mit Wagner und teilweise schon vor ihm haben viele Komponisten in der symphonischen Musik mit „charakteristischen" Motiven gearbeitet, die dieselben Eigenschaften aufweisen[19]. Das Phänomen erscheint weniger verwunderlich, wenn man sich vergegenwärtigt, daß das Ideal einer Vereinigung oder gar Verschmelzung von Musik und Poesie zu den Leitgedanken des 19. Jahrhunderts gehörte. Die musikalischen Konzeptionen mehrerer Komponisten entzündeten sich an der Literatur. Robert Schumann arbeitete an der Poetisierung der Instrumentalmusik, Hector Berlioz — der Schöpfer der dramatischen Symphonie — orientierte sich am Drama, und Franz Liszt schwebte das Ideal einer musikalischen Epik nach dem Muster der modernen „philosophischen" Epopöe Goethes und Byrons vor.

Einen der frühesten und wohl auch aufschlußreichsten Fälle für das Auftreten eines „charakteristischen" Motivs in der Programmusik stellt

---

[19] Die vorliegenden Erörterungen über „charakteristische" Motive basieren vorwiegend auf den Forschungsergebnissen meines Buches Gustav Mahler. Band II: Mahler und die symphonische Musik des 19. Jahrhunderts in neuer Deutung, Wiesbaden 1977. Von „charakteristischen Motiven" sprach übrigens Franz Liszt bereits im Jahre 1855. Siehe seinen Brief an Franz Brendel vom 18. März 1855.

die Symphonie fantastique von Hector Berlioz aus dem Jahre 1830 dar. Eine profilierte längere Melodie bildet den Hauptgedanken des Werkes und kehrt nach Art eines Leitfadens in allen fünf Sätzen wieder. Berlioz erläuterte sie programmatisch als den „melodischen Reflex" des Bildes der Geliebten, das einen jungen Künstler unausgesetzt verfolge. Dabei sprach er ausdrücklich von einer Idée fixe, einem Terminus, der bekanntlich dem Vokabular der Psychiatrie entlehnt ist. Die Idee der Besessenheit drückt in der Tat weiten Partien der Symphonie fantastique das Gepräge auf. Sie beherrscht nicht nur den Kopfsatz, sondern tönt auch in den anderen Sätzen auf, die den jungen Künstler in wechselnder Umgebung zeigen: mitten auf einem Ball, in einer Szene auf dem Lande, während des Marsches zum Schafott und schließlich in einer geträumten unheimlich-grotesken Szene, in der die Idée fixe ihren ursprünglichen teils leidenschaftlichen, teils vornehm-schüchternen Charakter verliert und in einer erstaunlichen Metamorphose als grell instrumentiertes triviales Tanzthema erscheint: das Bild der Geliebten weicht hier dem Bild einer hexenhaften Dirne. Mit der Idée fixe der Symphonie fantastique erschloß Berlioz der Musik eine tiefenpsychologische Dimension, die vielen seiner Zeitgenossen unheimlich bleiben mußte.

Berlioz' Idée fixe dürfte auf Peter Tschaikowsky einen starken Eindruck gemacht haben. Dessen 1888 entstandene Fünfte Symphonie dokumentiert nämlich, wie er Berlioz' Verfahren adaptierte und originell abwandelte. Die Symphonie wird mit einem rhythmisch prägnanten Thema eröffnet, das in allen Sätzen des Werkes wiederkehrt und sich dadurch als Leitthema erweist. Tschaikowsky verlieh ihm jedoch nicht die Semantik eines Liebesmotivs, sondern die eines Schicksalsgedankens. In Skizzen umschrieb er den Sinn der Introduktion mit den Worten: „Vollständige Beugung vor dem Schicksal, oder, was dasselbe ist, vor dem unergründlichen Walten der Vorsehung." Auch die Vierte Symphonie Tschaikowsky ist übrigens eine Schicksalssymphonie. In einem Brief verglich er das Schicksal mit einem Damoklesschwert, das über dem Haupte des Menschen schwebt und dessen Streben nach Glück vereitelt.

Das Schicksal, der Kampf, die Liebe, der Tod, die Ewigkeit, die Sehnsucht nach Erlösung, die postume Rehabilitierung der Verkannten und Unterdrückten, der postume Triumph großer Menschen und Ideen — das sind die großen Sujets in der Musik des 19. Jahrhunderts. Als Bausteine zu ihrer Darstellung und als vorantreibende Elemente fungieren die Leitmotive und die charakteristischen Motive. Besondere Beachtung unter ihnen verdienen zwei Urmotive bei Liszt, weil sie in seinem Schaffen eine zentrale Rolle spielen und auch bei anderen Komponisten rekurrieren. Gemeint sind das „tonische Symbol des Kreuzes" (eine gregorianische Wendung, die aus drei Tönen besteht) und der Tritonus, seit dem Mittelalter das Sinnbild des Satanischen in der Musik. Die beiden Urmotive stehen als polare Gegensätze an der Spitze der Lisztschen Symbolhierarchie und charakterisieren die Polarität zweier unvereinbarer Prinzipen, die man mit den Begriffspaaren Heil und Unheil, Gut und Böse nur annähernd beschreiben kann. Liszt verstand den Crucifixus und im weiteren Sinn das Kreuz als Metaphern für das „göttliche Licht", die „Erlösung" und die „höchste Seligkeit", während ihm Satan der Inbegriff für die Finsternis, den Tod, die Verneinung und den Zweifel war.

Entsprechend den vielen Bedeutungsvarianten, die der Crucifixus für Liszt hatte, versinnbildlicht das „tonische Symbol des Kreuzes" in seiner Musik mehrere Konnotationen des Heilsgedankens: den heiligen Geist, den Frieden im Herrn, die Kreuzesstätte Jesu Christi, den Willen Gottes. Noch weiter ist das semantische Feld des negativen Pols. Liszt verwendet den Tritonus als Symbol des Unheils im weitesten Sinne, das heißt: als Emblem Luzifers, Mephistos und der Hölle überhaupt, als Symbol des Tartarus, der Verwünschung, der Kühnheit und des Leidens, des Leids und des Todes, der Trauer und Klage, als Sinnbild für das Gespenstische, Schauerliche, Ungeheuerliche, als Symbol des Rasens, des Zweifels, des Grabes und des bösen Omens.

Liszts kunsttheoretische, religiöse und philosophische Ideen haben auf seine Zeitgenossen eine mächtige Wirkung ausgeübt. Etliche seiner Kernmotive erregten die Aufmerksamkeit mehrerer seiner Komponistenkollegen, die sie in ihr Schaffen übernahmen. Die Übertragung erfolgt in einer Weise, daß man von Migration und Rekursivität wohl sprechen kann. So setzte Anton Bruckner das Lisztsche „tonische Symbol des Kreuzes" in seinen Symphonien und in seiner geistlichen Musik etlichemal mit religiöser Semantik ein. Peter Tschaikowsky nahm es in den Kopfsatz seiner Pathétique auf. Richard Wagner bildete aus ihm und aus einem weiteren Motiv (dem Dresdner Amen) eines der wichtigsten Motive im Parsifal: das Gralsmotiv. Und Gustav Mahler baute das Finale seiner Ersten Symphonie teilweise auf Motiven auf, die er der Dante-Symphonie Liszts und dem Parsifal Wagners entlehnte. Bezeichnenderweise trägt der Satz im Autograph die Überschrift: Dall' Inferno al Paradiso.

Überhaupt ist Gustav Mahler ein philosophierender Komponist gewesen. Wie jüngere Forschungen ergaben, machte er die persönlichen, weltanschaulichen und religiösen Fragen, die ihn bewegten, zu Sujets seiner Symphonien. Seine Programme verliehen zentralen Inhalten seiner Weltanschauung Ausdruck. So ist die Idee der Transzendenz, die Idee der Überwindung des Elends und Leids philosophischer Grundgedanke der Ersten Symphonie. Das Sujet der Zweiten Symphonie darf man als eschatologisch bezeichnen: Mahler hat durch die programmatische Konzeption des Werkes und durch Einbeziehung poetischer Texte mit den Mitteln der Musik eine Antwort zu geben versucht auf all die Fragen, um die sein Denken kreiste: die Fragen nach dem Sinn des Lebens und des Todes und nach dem endzeitlichen Zustand des Menschen und der Welt. Der Glaube, zu dem er sich dabei bekannte, ist ein sehr persönlich gefärbtes Credo an die Unsterblichkeit. Ein kosmologisches Sujet liegt dann der Dritten Symphonie zugrunde, die aus dem Boden der Mahlerschen Liebesphilosophie erwächst. Ein eschatologiches Sujet hat übrigens auch die Vierte Symphonie, bei deren Konzeption Meditationen über das „Leben nach dem Tode" Pate gestanden haben. Zentrale Sujets Mahlers sind die Idee des Durchbruchs, die Polarität zwischen Inferno und Paradiso, die Idee der als Caritas verstandenen ewigen Liebe und vor allem die Idee der Fortdauer der Existenz nach dem Tode — ein Goethescher Gedanke, der Mahler mächtig anzog und den er in seinen Werken immer aufs neue behandelte.

Zur symphonischen Darstellung dieser geistigen Welt bedient sich Mahler einer großen Anzahl charakteristischer Motive, die in einzelnen Symphonien oder sogar in seinem ganzen Schaffen wiederkehren, anders ausgedrückt: die er intra- oder intertextuell verwendet. Einige dieser Motive entlehnte er — wie angedeutet — Werken von Liszt und Wagner sowie anderer Komponisten. Die meisten Motive freilich erfand er selbst. Dabei stattete er sie mit einer außermusikalischen Semantik aus, die in den meisten Fällen mit Hilfe verschiedener Methoden eruierbar ist. Interessanterweise gebrauchte Mahler die Begriffe Motiv und Symbol synonym. So äußerte er in einem Gespräch mit seiner Freundin Natalie Bauer-Lechner: „Alle Verständigung zwischen dem Komponisten und dem Hörer beruht auf einer Konvention: daß der letztere dieses oder jenes Motiv oder musikalisches Symbol, oder wie man es sonst nennen mag, als den Ausdruck für diesen oder jenen Gedanken oder eigentlichen geistigen Inhalt gelten läßt." Und im Anschluß daran beklagte er sich darüber, daß die Menschen auf seine Tonsprache noch nicht eingegangen seien.

Besondere Beachtung verdient, daß als charakterische Motive bei Mahler nicht nur melodische Gestalten fungieren, sondern auch Harmonien, Akkorde, Rhythmen und bestimmte Idiophone. So kehren eine

bestimmte Akkordfolge und ein prägnanter Rhythmus in drei Sätzen der
Sechsten Symphonie als Fatalitätssymbole immer wieder, und sie sind es
auch, die am Ende des Finales, einer grauenhaften Vision des Untergan-
ges, das letzte Wort behalten. Nicht minder relevant ist die klangsymboli-
sche und leitmotivische Verwendung mancher Idiophone bei Mahler. So
symbolisiert das Tamtam vielfach den Todesbereich; die Glocken ver-
sinnbildlichen die Ewigkeit; das Glockenspiel dient in vielen Fällen als
Klangrequisit der musica angelica, und die Herdenglocken charakterisieren — nach Mahlers eigener Erläuterung — ein „verhallendes Erdenge-
räusch", das der „auf höchstem Gipfel im Angesicht der Ewigkeit"
Stehende vernimmt.

<h1 style="text-align:center">VI</h1>

FOLGERUNGEN

Fassen wir die bisherigen Beobachtungen zusammen und berücksichti-
gen wir dabei die wichtige Frage nach der Vergleichbarkeit des musikalischen und des literarischen Motivbegriffs, so gelangen wir zu den
folgenden Ergebnissen:

1. Versucht man die verschiedenen Definitionen des musikalischen
Motivbegriffs auf eine Formel zu bringen, so ließe sich das Motiv als eine
stoffliche Einheit auffassen, die eine energetische Kraft hat und als
vorantreibendes Element wirkt.

2. Als besonders wichtig erweist sich die Unterscheidung zwischen
musikalischen Motiven ohne Semantik und solchen mit außermusikali-
scher Bedeutung. Letztere lassen sich am besten mit literarischen Motiven vergleichen. Leitmotive und charakteristische Motive erschließen
der Musik eine Dimension, die ihr von Haus aus nicht eigen ist: die
Dimension des Meinens. Dadurch wird Musik der Sprache ähnlich. Die
Musik des 19. Jahrhunderts steckt zu einem wesentlichen Teil voller
Intentionen.

3. Rekurrenz und Migration sind Erscheinungen, die sich auch beim
Studium der musikalischen Leitmotive und der charakteristischen Motive beobachten lassen. Bestimmte Kernmotive kehren im Schaffen einzel-
ner Komponisten wieder, und sie „wandern", in gleicher oder veränder-
ter Gestalt, in Werke anderer Komponisten. Leitmotive und charakteristische Motive erfüllen im Musikdrama und in der symphonischen
Musik des 19. Jahrhunderts vielfach eine psychologische Funktion, und

sie dienen als Bausteine zur Darstellung von Sujets von allgemeiner menschlicher Relevanz.

4. Als charakteristische Motive fungieren in der Musik nicht nur melodische Gestalten, sondern auch Akkordfolgen, prägnante Rhythmen und idiophonische Klangsymbole. Ungezählte Beispiele dafür lassen sich aus der Musik des 19. und auch des 20. Jahrhunderts anführen.

5. In der Literaturwissenschaft wird oft zwischen primären und sekundären Motiven unterschieden oder zwischen Kern-, Rahmen- und Füllmotiven. Ähnliche Unterscheidungen lassen sich auch im musikalischen Bereich treffen. Auch für die Erscheinung der Verknüpfung mehrerer literarischer Motive gibt es in der Musik ungezählte Parallelbeispiele, ja, man kann sagen, daß die Gegenüberstellung und Kombination der Leitmotive und der charakteristischen Motive im Musikdrama und in der symphonischen Musik die Regel bildet. So erwächst die Dynamik der Musik im Finale der Ersten Symphonie von Gustav Mahler aus dem Widerstreit zwischen den Inferno- und den Paradiso-Motiven, und ähnlich verhält es sich im Finale der Zweiten Symphonie von Mahler, wo Dies irae- und Auferstehungsmotive miteinander konfrontiert werden.

6. Manche Literaturwissenschaftler sondern scharf die literarischen Leitmotive von den „echten" Motiven. Nach Elisabeth Frenzel[20] sind Leitmotive „keine Bestandteile des Inhalts, keine echten Motive, sie sind auch keineswegs ‚leitend', sondern stilistische, tektonische, gliedernde Elemente, die eine Art musikalischen Effekt haben und einem Refrain gleichen". Eine ähnliche scharfe Unterscheidung zwischen Leitmotiven und charakteristischen Motiven läßt sich in der Musik nicht treffen. Beide Motivgruppen weisen annähernd die gleichen Eigenschaften auf. Allenfalls ließe sich sagen, daß musikdramatische Leitmotive im Gegensatz zu den charakteristischen Motiven mitunter etwas Plakatives haben.

7. Manche Literaturwissenschaftler räumen ein, daß viele Motive Symbolkraft haben, warnen jedoch vor einer Identifizierung der Begriffe Motiv und Symbol[21]. Unbestreitbar ist, daß zumal in der Lyrik symbolische Motive vorkommen und daß viele musikalische Leitmotive und charakteristische Motive Symbolcharakter haben. Überhaupt will es scheinen, als tendiere die Musik noch stärker zur symbolischen Gestaltung als die Literatur.

---

[20] Elisabeth Frenzel: Stoff-, Motiv- und Symbolforschung (1978), S. 34.
[21] Frenzel, ebenda, S. 30.

Eric DE KUYPER
(Katholieke Universiteit Nijmegen)

DE DUBBEL- OF MEERZINNIGHEID VAN MOTIEVEN EN FIGUREN

Vooraf

In deze bijdrage zullen we een poging ondernemen om met behulp van de greimasiaanse semiotiek een beknopt overzicht te geven van de stand van zaken op het gebied van het motievenonderzoek en om de algemene lijnen van een mogelijk werkperspectief aan te geven.

Omdat hun referentiële illusie centraal staat, lijken motieven en figuren doorzichtig, aantrekkelijk en geschikt voor analyse en theorievorming. Er is echter een ingewikkelde functioneringsstrategie nodig om die illusie tot stand te brengen, denken we maar aan theatrale illusies die het gevolg kunnen zijn van een sterk gecodificeerde en subtiele strategie.

Kenmerken en gevolgen

De *figuur*, '(...) unité à la fois plus petite et plus profonde de chacun des plans (du signifiant et du signifié) pris séparément' (A.J. Greimas, 1973, 169), wordt gekenschetst door zijn virtualiteit. Wanneer hij wordt gerealiseerd in een tekst, blijven buiten de tekst ontelbare mogelijkheden virtueel aanwezig. De gerealiseerde figuur kan een grote lading meekrijgen door een woekering van betekenissen, (...) figures du monde (rejetées) mais qui continuent à vivre leur existence virtuelle, prêtes à ressusciter au moindre effort de mémorisation.' (A.J. Greimas, 1973, 170).

Naast hun veelzijdigheid en hun virtuele meerzinnigheid hebben ze nog een andere karakteristiek: ze zijn geneigd zich te vermenigvuldigen, en in relatie te treden met andere figuren om zodoende gehelen te vormen die we *configuraties* noemen. Zulke configuraties leiden een min of meer *autonoom* bestaan, het zijn kleine verhaaltjes, 'micro-récits', 'cela veut dire qu'une configuration n'est pas dépendante de son contexte, qu'elle peut en être extraite et manifestée sous forme d'un discours autosuffisant' (A.J. Greimas, J. Courtès, 1979,60). Hun autonomie wordt echter afgezwakt doordat ze zich enten op het narratieve discours van de tekst waarin ze opgenomen worden en functioneren. Het autonome aspect van de configuraties wordt traditioneel aangeduid met de term *'motief'*.

78

De dubbele status van de configuraties (resp. de motieven) als varianten en invarianten heeft twee gevolgen:
— als 'micro-récit' kunnen ze aan een narratieve analyse onderworpen worden: '(...) leur manifestation discursive présuppose déjà une organisation narrative sous-jacente.' (A.J. Greimas, J. Courtès, 1979, 60)
— door hun koppeling met de narratieve structuur gaan ze deel uitmaken van de tekst en ook dit maakt hen toegankelijk voor een narratieve analyse. De verstrengeling van configuraties met de narratieve structuur van de tekst gebeurt via de zgn. rollen (actantiële of figuratieve) (A.J. Greimas, J. Courtès, 1979, 318 en 60).

We dienen hierbij ook oog te hebben voor de geactualiseerde waarden die in het thema tot uiting komen. In een filmtekst als 'Ossessione' van L. Visconti[1] worden bijvoorbeeld bepaalde waarden geactualiseerd in de thema's van het 'zwerven' en 'zich vestigen'. Op hun beurt worden deze thema's gefigurativiseerd in de beelden van het 'bed' en de 'weg'. Het thema van het zwerven wordt in eerste instantie gefigurativiseerd in de 'weg', maar is ook aanwezig in het 'bed' en omgekeerd wordt het thema van het 'zich vestigen' vervlochten met de 'weg'. Dit heeft te maken met het spel der waarden dat hier op een specifieke manier geïdeologiseerd wordt in de organisatie van homosexualiteit/heterosexualiteit.

Idiolectale en sociolectale semantische universums

De organisatie van de axiologie (semantische waardeleer) in een ideologie kan zowel idiolectaal als sociolectaal zijn. Niet alleen binnen de tekst maar ook daarbuiten zijn ideologieën aanwezig die niet noodzakelijk met elkaar hoeven overeen te stemmen. Zo vertoont de film L'Atalante van Jean Vigo[2] op het ideologische vlak wel overeenkomsten met het surrealisme, terwijl hij er op het figuratieve vlak sterk van afwijkt. In Ossessione wijkt de ideologie zelfs in sterke mate af van de sociolectale ideologie van het neo-realisme. We kunnen vier dimensies onderscheiden in de ideologische organisatie van de filmtekst: twee (idiolectaal en sociolectaal) binnen de tekst en twee daarbuiten.

Intra-tekstueel en extra-tekstueel

Dankzij het onderscheid tussen de intra-tekstuele en de extra-tekstuele dimensies krijgen we een scherper inzicht in de hele problematiek van de

---

[1] Dit opstel herneemt een vorige tekst en refereert aan voorbeelden die aldaar uitvoeriger besproken werden.
[2] E. de Kuyper, Het onverwachte «surrealisme» van Jean Vigo's l'Atalante', verschenen in Versus, 1986.

figuren, motieven en thema's. Op deze manier kan immers een socio-historische en een socio-culturele dimensie binnen de tekst worden teruggevonden. Het zou dus totaal inconsequent zijn te beweren dat de tekstuele analyse geen aandacht heeft voor 'historische', 'sociale', 'persoonlijke' en 'stilistische' aspecten. Evenmin heeft het zin te pleiten voor een verruiming van de tekstanalyse door meer aandacht te schenken aan voornoemde dimensies los van de eigenlijke tekst. Deze dimensies zijn immers al aanwezig in de tekst zelf en met name in de figuren en de thema's die nauw verbonden zijn met het semantisch universum. Het is nochtans wel nodig om de verschillende dimensies beter tot hun recht te laten komen in de tekst. De studie van de werking van thema's en figuren vormt daartoe het aangewezen middel.

Extratekstualiteit als intertekstualiteit

Om de problematiek rondom de socio-culturele dimensie(s) van de tekst op een zinvolle manier te benaderen volstaat het niet dat we het bestaan van de extra-tekst erkennen. We dienen ook te beseffen dat de extra-tekst geen vacuüm vormt, maar zelf georganiseerd wordt door een groot aantal tekstuele systemen die niet noodzakelijk van visuele, audio-visuele of verbale aard zijn.

Wanneer we naar aanleiding van *Ossessione* stellen dat het thema respectievelijk het motief van de 'weg' (la strada') belangrijk is voor het Italiaanse neo-realisme, dan is het nodig dat we het begrip 'Italiaans neo-realisme' in een tekstuele vorm gieten zodat de koppeling tussen *Ossessione* (tekst I) en het Italiaans neo-realisme (tekst II) duidelijk wordt. Het gaat niet meer om extra-tekstualiteit, maar ol intertekstualiteit.

Wanneer we semiotische systemen van verschillende grootte en aard op elkaar willen afstemmen, hebben we niet genoeg aan verwijzingen naar een lexicon van thema's en motieven. Elk van de betrokken systemen bezit immers een eigen grammatica.

Angst en geruststelling

We zijn uitgegaan van eenvoudige gegevens als motieven en thema's die vaak tot stereotiepen, clichés en platitudes worden. Wanneer we hun werking binnen en buiten de tekst willen analyseren, merken we evenwel

---

[3] Voor de film heeft Ch. Metz het probleem van de diversiteit in grootheid besproken in het hoofdstuk getiteld «Textes filmiques plus grands ou plus petits qu'un film», in: Ch. Metz, *Langage et Cinéma*, Paris, 1971, p. 91 e.v.

[4] Zie noot 2.

dat het hele semiotische bouwwerk in beweging komt. De socio-semiotische en psychosemiotische dimensies die hiermee verbonden zijn werden nog maar weinig onderzocht.

Door hun heterogeniteit hebben bepaalde soorten niet-verbale teksten, — zoals bijvoorbeeld films — vrijwel onbeperkte mogelijkheden om configuraties op te roepen. R. Barthes kan in *S/Z* de werking van de figuren in een bepaalde novelle van Balzac pas op het spoor komen nadat hij het werk aan een diepgaande analyse heeft onderworpen. Bij filmische teksten met hun audio-visuele verstrengelingen en hun referentiële rijkdom wordt het allemaal nog veel moeilijker. Alle elementen die zich in een filmische tekst manifesteren kunnen onderzocht worden op hun 'figurativiteit'[5].

Filmische teksten zijn in alle opzichten complexer dan literaire. R. Jakobson verklaarde ooit eens dat hij zich nauwelijks semiotiek kon voorstellen zonder dat de filmsemiotiek daarin een centrale plaats zou bekleden. De problemen geven echter zelf hun eigen oplossing aan. Wie zich met filmsemiotiek bezighoudt beseft al snel dat de eerste regel van de semiotische analyse bestaat in het zuivere, relevante functioneren van de tekens. Sedert Hjelmslev weten we dat de onderzoeker zelf zijn object constitueert. Daartoe worden we nu net gedwongen wanneer we met de problematiek rondom figuren en motieven in de filmsemiotiek worden geconfronteerd.

Literatuur
A.J. GREIMAS, *Les Actants, les Acteurs et les Figures*, in: C. CHABROL (ed.), *Sémiotique Narrative et Textuelle*, Paris, 1973.
A.J. GREIMAS, J. COURTES, *Sémiotique. Dictionnaire raisonné de la Théorie du Langage*, Paris, 1979.

[5] Terloops heb ik in mijn artikel (noot 1) erop gewezen dat de geselecteerde configuraties van «bed» en «weg» nog van vele andere configuraties doordrongen zijn.